PURPOSE IN EVERY PAYCHECK

PURPOSE
IN EVERY
PAYCHECK

DISCOVER FINANCIAL FREEDOM
AND THE FUTURE YOU'RE MADE FOR

KYLE BLACKWELL, CFP®

Streamline
BOOKS

To my Lord and Savior, Jesus Christ. Through a season of discontent, you ignited a holy ambition in me to share what I've learned from your Word about faithful stewardship and how your timeless principles are just as impactful for today's generation.

To my wife, my partner since our freshman year of high school. Your constant love and support steady me, and I fall deeper in love with you every single day.

To my daughter, whose passion for reading sparked the inspiration for this book. Your God-given curiosity and creativity shine brightly, and I know you'll use them to glorify him.

To my son, whose relentless grit and boundless compassion—like a honey badger with a heart for hugs—push me to strive to be a better man.

CONTENTS

INTRODUCTION

GROWING UP IN AN OUT-OF-CONTROL WORLD

I t's a Saturday morning: time to relax after a long week. You open up your social media app of choice. Before you even have a chance to take a first sip of coffee, your brain's been flooded with something like this:

- An ad for fancy, limited-edition shoes—oh man, the compliments you'd get on these. (Sure, they're expensive, and who knows if they're comfortable? But that "buy now, pay later" offer seals the deal.)
- A reel from a confident cryptobro who wants to tell you (or sell you?) his secret to making millions and retiring in your twenties.
- Some perfectly staged photos of a distant relative's enormous, stylish house. Seriously, how on *earth* is he affording all that?
- An influencer's video on today's viral beauty trend. It's a nonstop humble brag, and you gawk at the price tag on each of the products she holds up for the camera.

- ◆ Inspirational words from a LinkedIn lunatic: a breakdown of how their daily cold plunges and skipped lattes propelled them to success and why you should be just like them.

It's an onslaught. You're still in your pajamas, but you're already clicking Buy Now, wrestling with envy, researching the stock market, and having a full-blown existential crisis. Sound fun?

Or, more to the point, sound familiar?

I don't need to lay this out in too much detail because you're the one living it: you've grown up with the constant background noise of ads and credit card offers, pulled between headlines about layoffs and the newest, youngest millionaires, all while social media pumps steroids into the materialistic human tendency to compare and compete.

Now you're hitting adulthood, and as you tackle the hard work of making and dealing with your own money, you realize no one ever even sat you down and walked you through the basics of budgeting and wise financial management. How do you do this adulting thing when it comes to money—and do it the *right* way in such a money-obsessed world?

A COMMON STORY

I didn't come from money by any means. No one gave me thorough, solid financial guidance when I was young, but I went out of my way to find it.

The analytical side of the stock market and economic trends fascinated me from an early age. I bought my first stock in middle school, and by freshman year of high school, I was reading magazines like *Kiplinger* and *Barron's* and telling people I wanted to be a stock broker when I grew up. I majored in business and accounting during college, cofounded an investment club, and interned at a myriad of financial planning firms. When I stepped straight out of school and into a career in financial advising, I discovered that I could always grind a bit harder, pick up another client or two, and make financial success just *happen* for myself.

That still didn't mean I knew what to *do* with that success once I attained it.

The satisfaction I felt at being a high earner was immense. I'm embarrassed to admit how often I gave myself a little pat on the back while comparing myself against people I'd known in high school or college. While so many others from my hometown and social circles were still just muddling through, my wife and I spent our twenties traveling the world together. We ticked things off our bucket list like we were about to die any day. It was fun. And it was fleeting.

It didn't take long for the self-satisfied thought *I'm doing pretty good for myself* to turn into a question: *Can everyone tell how well I'm doing?* It wasn't enough to just be successful; I wanted to make sure other people *knew* I was successful.

One day, my wife came home, saying, "Have you seen So-and-so's house? He must make a *ton*." I knew the guy. I knew for a fact that I made more money than him, but, yeah, his house *was* nicer than ours. So was his car. He *looked* more successful than me. Pretty soon after that, we bought a bigger house. But not a fancier car, simply because I'm not a car guy. I only recently bought a more high-end vehicle for the first time, but exclusively because I like the tech involved, *not* out of any interest in learning how to tinker with it. To paraphrase an old Jeff Foxworthy joke: if you ever find me under a car, call 911 because that is *not* a natural place for me to be. (Even now that I have a nicer car, I paid cash for it and didn't buy new. But more on that in a later chapter.)

I thought my wife would be proud of me. I thought we'd earned it and that we deserved a life of comfort. We had a pool. We had way too many bedrooms and bathrooms for what was now a family of four. Heck, we had a bounce house in one of those extra rooms. That's how extra it all was.

One day I stood in our basement, staring into several empty rooms that we couldn't even fill, and I felt an incredible weight of guilt. What was I *doing*? What was I chasing? Whatever it was, it hadn't paid off. I felt empty, and I couldn't do it anymore.

I'm now seventeen years into my career as a financial advisor. From my own personal experience and from observing my clients, I can tell you that the rat race has only gotten nastier since I started chasing success, and our standards have only gotten higher. A 2024 poll by Empower shows that while members of older generations (Boomers, Gen X, and millennials) consider a salary between \$100,000–\$200,000 enough to make someone "financially successful," members of Gen Z wouldn't assign that label to anything less than nearly \$600,000.[1] Read that again. Six. Hundred. Thousand.

In reality? The average US salary in 2025, across generations, is just \$66,600.[2] Talk about a disconnect.

There's nothing wrong with shooting for success. But is success just dollars and cents? The ability to buy whatever you want with a single click, to lord your achievements over your old friends at the next high school reunion, to relax in the knowledge that you've got assets to keep you safe and secure for the next two hundred years?

Or is it something more?

LISTENING TO THE WHISPER

If you grew up in church, chances are there's a whisper in the back of your mind, struggling to make itself heard through the consumeristic chaos and money, money, money narrative of this world: a whisper about generosity, love of neighbor, humility, wise stewardship, and an identity grounded in something much bigger and deeper than wealth or success. Will you spend some time with me—phone aside, background noise off—to listen to that whisper today?

All that time ago, when I stood looking at the wasteful emptiness of my house, I knew something had to change. I didn't have to chase down "enough" for my family anymore; we had *more* than enough. There was no more satisfaction to be had there. So what was next?

I found my answer in the Bible, in service, and in my identity as a steward of God's gracious gifts. We sold that great big house for a smaller one, one that fit the family's needs and felt like a home to be used instead of a showcase to be admired. I stopped focusing on rewards and started focusing on my clients and how I might best serve them. I started volunteering with a group that plays adaptive pickleball, coming alongside a group of wonderful people with special needs, and filled my days with meaning that had absolutely nothing to do with money. This book was written to share some of the lessons I learned along the way: big ones around identity and service and community and nitty-gritty ones about budgets and credit cards and meme stocks.

The heart of it all? How to handle money God's way.

The world wants us to get our wants and our needs mixed up. The world wants us to choose comfort over honoring God, but that second, harder path is the better one every time by a factor of about a billion.

What's it look like to handle money God's way exactly? Let's dive in together.

Part 1

THE DISCONNECT

Chapter 1

DISLOCATED IDENTITY

*Spiritual identity means we are not what we do or what people say about us.
And we are not what we have. We are the beloved daughters and sons of God.*

—HENRI NOUWEN

THE EMOTIONAL AND SPIRITUAL WEIGHT OF MONEY

What does money mean to you?

When you linger on that word—*money*—what starts happening in your mind and body? Do you get hit by a wave of anxiety, thrown straight into that hold-your-breath feeling of checking your bank account to make sure you'll have enough this month? Or maybe you get a boost of adrenaline thinking of the overtime you could work, the extra sales or clients you could take on, the side hustle you could dive into—because you've had a taste, and you want more.

Oftentimes, our baseline beliefs about money are formed by our upbringings: by how those closest to us when we were children and teens handled that green paper or plastic card. If you grew up in a family that experienced financial hardship, you probably have memories of seeing your parents or guardians in the thick of visceral, intense levels of stress. That kind of instability and worry is bound to plant a seed in a child, a seed that says that money is an extremely important, extremely scarce resource. On the other hand, if you grew up getting pretty much every-thing you asked for, living in an upscale neighborhood and taking fancy vacations, chances are you thought money was no big deal, something that just grew on trees.

So that's where it starts. Our early beliefs about money are shaped by what we see around us growing up.

But it doesn't stop there. Who are you closest to today? Or, put an-other way, who are you most influenced by? Who has the attention of your eyes and ears?

I suggest you start answering this question by taking a look at your phone's screen time tracker (and if you've never done that before, prepare to be shocked). We live in an era of 24/7 access: access to social media, to anything we could possibly want to Google, to all our favorite shows, to online discourse and online shopping. It's all at our fingertips, and that's a blessing and a curse. Sure, the world of our phones offers entertain-ment, information, convenience, and sometimes, community. But it also offers boundless temptations and opportunities to fall into greed, envy, vanity—heck, any and all of the deadly sins you care to imagine. And it has a deep and lasting effect on how we think about and use our money.

We all have an innate tendency to mimic. Hang out with a group of friends who all talk a certain way or have a certain kind of humor for long enough, and it'll rub off on you. Studies show that the younger we are, the more susceptible we are to being swayed by others, and overall, that's just part of being human. The influencers and marketers on your phone know it, too. Every time you look at your screen, you're being hit with product-packed GRWM reels, targeted ads, social media's comparison trap, FOMO, enticing (but dicey) information about how to become a millionaire fast, and so much more. You want to be like the people you see, these people who set the tone and the vibe, and whether their content prompts you to click Buy or not, those ideas—about what's important and meaningful, what it looks like to be a thriving human living "the good life," how to be happy and successful—they all sink in and settle somewhere deep.

Of course, the exploitation of the human tendency to mirror what we see is nothing new. Back in the 1920s, cigarette companies decided they'd had enough of the social taboo around women smoking—not because they particularly cared about the rights of women, but because they looked at all these nonsmoking adults and saw a potential goldmine. Previously, smoking was seen as an exclusively male habit; women who *did* smoke were considered immoral and corrupt. Before cigarette companies could make a profit off this whole new market, they had to shift the social perception of the idea. So what did they do? They branded cigarettes "torches of freedom," made them a symbol of female emancipation, and then hired good-looking women to smoke their "torches of freedom" and walk in the 1929 Easter Sunday Parade in New York. It sparked a conversation and made the act of smoking a political statement, and cigarette sales rocketed up among women.[3] Monkey see; monkey do.

Marketing tends to be a bit sneakier today, and most of it happens online, but it still appeals to that human desire to imitate those around us: to be cool, to be a part of a greater movement or community, or to just be "normal" like everyone else. Those pulls have been intensified astronomically because they're pervasive in the space where we willingly put our eyes and minds for hours each day. Add that digital saturation to the reality that today's generations of teens and young adults are frequently growing up with emotional struggles—in broken homes, with physical and mental health challenges, or just under the pressures of what they perceive to be an unstable world and future. Then, add the fact that so few of our young people today were given a solid education in financial management, either from guardians or their schools, and you've got yourself a tsunami.

As you will learn in this book, how you view and interact with money has a profound effect on your life. So, if you take your cue from how the world views and interacts with money, your life will resemble that of the average person. Want to guess what that means? Well, credit card debt is skyrocketing in the United States; at the time of this writing, Americans have a whopping $1.211 trillion in unpaid credit card debt.[4] Thirty-seven percent of Americans today report having been diagnosed with a mental health condition like anxiety or depression, and a full third feel that they have too much stress in their day-to-day lives to think about the future at all.[5] Sound like something you want to aspire toward?

According to Galatians 5:19–21 (MSG), the world can only offer us stuff like this:

> *Repetitive, loveless, cheap sex; a stinking accumulation of mental and emotional garbage; frenzied and joyless grabs for happiness; trinket gods; magic-show religion; paranoid loneliness; cutthroat competition; all-consuming-yet-never-satisfied wants; a brutal temper; an impotence to love or be loved; divided homes and divided lives; small-minded and lopsided pursuits; the vicious habit of depersonalizing everyone into a rival; uncontrolled and uncontrollable addictions; ugly parodies of community.*

"Oh no," I can hear you saying, "is this going to be the kind of book that tells us the world is garbage and the only way to serve God and live well is through joyless asceticism?" Don't worry: I get it. My goal in writing this book isn't to take the fun out of living—quite the contrary. My goal is to help you identify your current beliefs about money, understand what God says about it compared to what the world says, and hopefully inspire you to take action toward having a healthy relationship with it so that you will live a life of lasting joy instead of fleeting happiness. Because money can hijack your thoughts, actions, and your overall life if you let it. It can take you over, and it all starts with looking to the wrong source for our sense of identity.

WHO TELLS US WHO WE ARE?

Personally, I spent most of my life with my identity all wrapped up in *what I do.*

I already shared my story of the envy and grinding for success that prompted me to buy a bigger house than I could ever possibly need. But even before that foolishness had set in, I was busy chasing down my identity in the form of *performance.*

Identity: Who we are—really.

I was a baseball player in high school, so that was my goal for college: to keep that identity by playing ball at the college level. When I met that goal, my self-worth was off the charts. After a year of playing and two shoulder injuries, though, the dream ended, my self-worth dropped, and honestly, I didn't even really know who I was anymore, if not a baseball player. So what did I do? Shot straight to my next identity source at super speed. This time, it came in the form of a career.

For the next decade and a half, I saw myself primarily as a financial planner and businessman. A Christian one, sure, but that wasn't exactly something I placed at the forefront. I'd been a believer since I was seven, so I always had the head knowledge that my identity was found in Jesus and Jesus alone, but I did not make a conscious, purposeful decision to let my faith define my sense of self or my daily actions. Instead, my work dictated how I felt about myself. While my business thrived, I knew exactly who I was, and I had a high sense of self-worth. But even that mountaintop experience would end with a wake-up call. I can tell you now, looking back: placing my identity in success and performance did not pay off even a tiny bit.

If we mimic the world and place our identities in something external, like we're told to do—in our job and our image, or a relationship, or our money and possessions—then our sense of self-worth ebbs and flows with the successes and failures of those transient things.

Got a promotion at work? Cool, here's some nice, high self-worth. But hang on: there's a round of layoffs, and you're out on the curb? Great, now your self-worth is rock bottom. Or as another example: got a fancy new car you're super proud of? Yay, self-worth. But hang on. Your best friend got an even nicer one? Dang, back in the dumps for you.

In *Stop Trying*, Cary Schmidt puts it well:

> *Our psyches are glued-together bits of not-built-to-last materials —health, looks, income, status, ethnicity, accomplishments, relationships, and social media profiles. We are*

perpetually haunted by comparison, the opinions of others,
competition, and fear. We are forever trying to measure up
to the world around us. When we do, we feel good. When
we fail, we feel loss.[6]

How do you define yourself today? Where do you turn for acceptance, security, and significance? Who's telling you who you are, and are you listening? Is it the socialites and influencers and TikTok success stories? Is it your paycheck, possessions, and performance? Or is it God?

GROUNDED IN A DEEPER TRUTH

Remember that passage from Galatians 5 about what the world offers us? As Paul continues in Galatians 5:22–24 (MSG), here's what happens when we live God's way instead:

> *He brings gifts into our lives, much the same way that fruit*
> *appears in an orchard—things like affection for others, ex-*
> *uberance about life, serenity. We develop a willingness to*
> *stick with things, a sense of compassion in the heart, and a*
> *conviction that a basic holiness permeates things and peo-*
> *ple. We find ourselves involved in loyal commitments, not*
> *needing to force our way in life, able to marshal and direct*
> *our energies wisely.*

We are not what we do, own, or achieve. We are human *beings*, not human *doings*. Only God offers an identity that isn't fragile, and only his words can direct us down the right paths. Everything else is fragile, inconsistent, and short-lived, but God is immovable, unshakable, and everlasting, the same yesterday, today, and forever. *That* is an identity worth buying into.

When we find ourselves by looking around horizontally, at the people and culture and created things we're embedded in, trying to find hope and peace and meaning there, we stumble. When we find ourselves by looking vertically, toward God, building our relationship with him above all else, we find true stability. And when we are rooted in God's unchanging love and purpose—what Cary Schmidt calls "Gospel identity"[7]—a byproduct is the fruits described in the passage above. Even more than that, being rooted in God gives us lasting acceptance, security, and significance.

Matthew 6:24 tells us that we cannot serve both God and money. To rediscover our identities in our eternal, all-powerful God, we must surrender: we must trust that God will meet our needs and give us the strength to endure any hardship, and we must choose contentment and gratitude *no matter what.*

Where does that surrender start? With resting in our identities in God by releasing our finances into his hands, stepping firmly into the truth that he owns it all anyway. Let's begin there.

Focus Questions

1. What were the spoken or unspoken messages about money in your home growing up? How do you think those messages have shaped your beliefs or behaviors today?
2. When you think about money, what emotions come up first? Why do you think that is?
3. Who has the most influence over how you think about success, identity, and money? Are these voices helping you grow closer to God—or pulling you toward comparison and consumerism?
4. How does your screen time (social media, online shopping, influencers, etc.) affect your self-perception and financial choices? Is there a disconnect between what you say you value and what you're absorbing?

Do It Today

1. Look through your phone's screen time tracker. What apps dominate your attention? What messages are those apps sending you

about money, identity, and success? Set one screen boundary for the next seven days—whether it's deleting an app, turning off notifications, or limiting time—and notice how it affects your thoughts around money and identity.

2. Write a list of "I am..." statements based on where you currently find identity (e.g., "I am a good student," "I am an athlete," "I am 'the funny one'"). Now rewrite a new list of "I am..." statements grounded in what God says about you. Use Scripture if helpful (e.g., "I am God's beloved," "I am chosen," "I am not what I do").

Chapter 2

GOD OWNS IT ALL

Every faculty you have, your power of thinking or of moving your
limbs from moment to moment, is given you by God. If you devoted
every moment of your whole life exclusively to His service you could
not give Him anything that was not in a sense His already.

— C. S. LEWIS

LEARNING THROUGH EXPERIENCE: REDEFINING SUCCESS

Success has nothing to do with houses or cars, but it has everything to do with the heart. I learned that at the very beginning of my career.

I built my business the old-fashioned way: by knocking on doors. I was twenty-two at the time and looked even younger, so I'll forever be grateful that doorbell cameras weren't yet common—it's easier to ignore someone's knock if you can observe and evaluate them while staying unseen yourself, and I suspect a lot more people would have left the door unanswered if they'd been able to take a secret peek at me. I'm sure many would have made the assumption I was selling Krispy Kremes for the local high school.

Those were interesting days. Ninety-degree temperatures, and there I was dragging myself around a cul-de-sac dressed in a stylishly oversized suit. I learned a lot: not to turn my back on a growling dog (I still have a ripped pair of old pants to remind me of that one), and not to let one unhappy person ruin your day (I once knocked on the door of a man who threatened to shoot me, then proceeded to mock me off the porch—but I didn't quit that day, and wound up meeting one of my best long-term clients a few doors over).

But the biggest lesson learned from my door-knocking days was simple: don't judge a book by its cover.

It probably goes without saying that in the wealth management business, success depends on managing a significant amount of money. So when I set out to build a practice of my own, it made sense—at least on paper—to target people who looked like they *had* wealth. The big house in the new development, with a shiny Mercedes parked in the garage—jackpot, right?

Not quite.

Sure, some of those guys earned a lot. But they usually *spent* a lot too. I met corporate midlevel executives juggling a country club membership, two leased luxury cars, and a massive mortgage; and I met young doctors, still buried in med school debt, trying to "look the part" with extravagant vacations, social media–worthy purchases, and credit card bills that kept piling up.

Were they wealthy? Not even close. Many of them had a negative net worth. Net worth is your assets minus your liabilities—and in these cases, the liabilities (car loans, student loans, mortgages, credit cards) far outweighed the assets. By the time their high incomes hit their bank accounts, most of it was already spoken for. They were stressed, overextended, and had little to no savings—let alone investable assets for me to help them with. (Though in retrospect, I wish I'd had the knowledge and courage to offer those people some guidance, even if they weren't my ideal clients at the time.)

So then, what about the modest homes off the beaten path—the ones with older siding and a well-worn Toyota Camry in the driveway? No Benz, no country club membership—not exactly promising, right?

Wrong.

Often, these were the exact people who had quietly mastered two timeless principles of stewardship—principles found clearly in the Bible:

1. They honored God with their finances by tithing.
2. They lived within their means by consistently spending less than they earned.

Simple? Yes. Easy? Not at all. But those principles created financial margins that eventually led to time margins. These were the people who didn't have to work overtime to pay off debt. They weren't running on a hamster wheel to fund a lifestyle. They had savings. They had peace of mind. And when the time came, they just needed someone like me to help manage the money they had already worked so diligently to steward.

> **Margin:** Speaking financially, the difference between your expenses and your income; speaking in terms of time and capacity, the space between your load and your limits; that thing that gives you room to breathe.

They had no car payments because they'd paid cash for their cars years ago and drove them until it made sense to replace them. Many of them had fully paid-off homes, not because they struck it rich but because they made extra payments consistently and paid down their mortgages early. If they wanted to remodel the kitchen, they didn't take out a home equity loan. They saved and waited. (Yes, waited. Remember when people used to do that?)

These people weren't trying to keep up with the Joneses. They were playing their own game, focused on family, church, and community. Their wealth wasn't flashy, but it was real. And I helped them grow their savings through investing, reduce their tax burden by placing money in the right types of accounts, and guide their kids and grandkids so those values of wise stewardship could live on.

So don't judge a book by its cover or a person's worth by their house or car. The real measure of success is wise stewardship, not lifestyle.

And that wise stewardship begins with the simple acknowledgment that everything we think we own is really, actually, God's.

Stewardship: A way of approaching "our" money, knowing that God is the true owner of all our resources, not us. And so we are called to **manage his gifts wisely,** with his glory and the love of our neighbors at the forefront.

A BIBLICAL UNDERSTANDING OF STEWARDSHIP

Jesus spoke about money more than sex, heaven, or hell. Why? Because it can so easily become your master if you're not careful. As Jesus says in Matthew 6:24, *"No one can serve two masters. Either you will hate the one and love the other, or you will be devoted to the one and despise the other. You cannot serve both God and money."*

If you would rather serve, love, and be devoted to God instead of money (and I pray that you do), you first need to understand that your master, God, owns it all—yes, even "your" money.

Stewardship is the act of faithfully and responsibly managing all that God has given us. It's owning up to the fact that everything comes from God: that it's his, not ours. That means our money, our time, our relationships, our bodies, our talents, anything that is God's creation (so, everything) *all belong to him.* We don't own anything; we only manage it.

It almost sounds trite to say that, and if you grew up in the church, you've heard it said before. But can we take a second to really let it sink in? Your home is not yours. Your skills are not yours. Your health is not yours. Your days are not yours. Your money is not yours. They're all God's. And if the Parable of the Talents tells us anything, it's that God expects us to use his gifts *wisely.* He wants us to act with accountability, honoring our purpose as his hands and feet on this earth. As 1 Peter 4:10 puts it, *"Each of you should use whatever gift you have received to serve others, as faithful stewards of God's grace in its various forms."*

That's it. We're here to serve others with the gifts God gave us—with our everything.

After all, it's not ours. It's God's. And do you really feel OK with the idea of wasting something that belongs to the maker of the universe? Blowing it all on meaningless pleasures? Engaging with life thoughtlessly, selfishly, every day on repeat till it ends?

I hope not. I hope you're ready to step into who you truly were made to be: a steward.

Remember our previous chapter when we talked about how many of today's problems stem from us trying to find our identities in the wrong things? God is the only true, stable identity source out there. He tells us we are his beloved children, and he tells us we are stewards.

STEWARDSHIP IN A MISMANAGED WORLD

As we've already discussed, a high income does not create true wealth—especially if it's accompanied by high debt. In my mind, the true indicator of financial thriving is plain old margin. It's being able to breathe easy, not because you earn hundreds of thousands of dollars and throw it all at the high life of your dreams but because you manage whatever amount you earn responsibly and well.

Now, am I saying it's sinful to earn a hefty salary? No. But check your motives. Whether you're living paycheck to paycheck or successfully climbed your way up the corporate ladder till you could buy a private island out of pocket if you wanted to, you don't get to treat your money frivolously or even like it's yours to do what you want with. It's God's. Treat it like what it is: a loan you're expected to use for good.

Proverbs 12:15 tells us: *"The way of fools seems right to them, but the wise listen to advice."* So, where are you getting your advice from? God's good Word? Or this crazy mismanaged world, where instant gratification is the norm, everyone's trying to keep up with the Joneses, and everybody's in debt?

In a world where you're told it's all yours for the taking, it's yours, and you deserve it, listen to the quieter, true voice of the Creator in the midst of the social static, the voice calling you toward wisdom and service.

MORE THAN JUST DOLLARS

As a high-achieving, competitive person, working hard to build my business at the beginning of my career came naturally to me. The financial services industry is fast-paced and full of rejection—but if you keep your head down, treat people well, and push through those early years with grit and consistency, the rewards do come.

My wife and I are both naturally frugal, so it didn't take long before we reached a level of financial comfort. But something unexpected began to creep in. Once the pressure lifted and the carrot chasing lost its appeal, I found myself slipping—not into contentment but into something a little more dangerous: complacency.

It caught me off guard. I'd worked so hard to build a business and reach that comfortable place, but now I was wrestling with the question: *What's next?* I wasn't driven by the next incentive trip or the next promotion anymore. And honestly, I didn't want to be. But I also knew I didn't want to coast. That's not who I was called to be.

Around that time, I had a conversation with a seasoned advisor—a veteran in the business who'd been through the same phase earlier in his career. He told me that when money stopped motivating him, the thing that re-centered him was a deeper understanding of stewardship.

At first, I brushed it off. *Stewardship? I'm already a good steward. I manage my money well. I give generously. I save wisely. I live within my means.*

But then he said something that stuck with me: "You've been given a gift—a unique ability to help people manage their money well. Don't waste that. Steward it. Use it fully, not for your own comfort, but to serve others in a way that honors God."

That moment reframed everything for me. It wasn't about growing my business just to hit another milestone—it was about faithfully managing *every* gift I'd been given. Stewardship wasn't just about handling money wisely; it was about stewarding my time, talents, influence, and energy. It was about bringing purpose back to the work.

And as crazy as it sounds, work became fun again. I showed up with more intention. I became a better advisor. And as a byproduct—not the goal but the fruit—my business grew.

All that to say, when I talk about stewarding God's good gifts well, I'm not just talking about money. Stewardship includes everything God gives us: our time, our skills, our relationships, our possessions, our energy, and our bodies.

Here's a silly little example of how easy it is to forget that call to be stewards of *everything* we've been given. We all get just one body to live in, maintain, strengthen, and use, right? When you think about it that way—just one body for the rest of our lives—it's a strong reminder that we should choose to treat those bodies properly and steward them well.

Many of us are in the good habit of blessing our food before we eat, and that's a great thing. I'm a firm believer in gratitude, in thanking God for providing food for me to eat, and I teach my kids to do the same. Every once in a while, I'll take my kids out for lunch and ice cream, and our go-to is Five Guys. Since Five Guys thinks highly of their burgers and fries, and charges accordingly, I like to get my money's worth: I eat the whole burger and the entire overflowing cup of fries when we're there.

One day, on one of these special outings, we were seated at the table, greasy burgers and Cajun-seasoned fries inches from our noses. We were salivating, but of course, we paused for our customary premeal blessing. Once the feast was over, we headed out for frozen yogurt. In a food coma already, we didn't bother asking God's blessing over our gummy-worm and chocolate-heaped dairy sweetness at that point. That's when it hit me: I personally believed God was maybe pretty glad we didn't insult his intelligence by asking his blessing over another helping of junk. I had an image of him looking over us, eyebrows up, chuckling, "What? You expect me to turn this into salmon and broccoli on its way down or something?"

So what am I saying? No burgers, no fries, no ice cream, no fun? Nah. Just like it's OK from time to time to spend money on fun, unnecessary things, feel free to please your taste buds (and expanding belly) on occasion. But moderation is key. Remember that you only have one body, and treat it as such. Because being a good steward is managing well *everything* that God has allowed us to manage.

Same goes for your time, your energy, your relationships, the stuff you own, and so much more. If you take nothing else from this book, hear this: slow down. Get thoughtful. Let every choice you make come from a place of wise, responsible stewardship. That's what we were put here for, and it really, truly matters.

STEWARDSHIP AS A WAY OF LIFE

My son's favorite animal is the honey badger.

Why? From a young age, I encouraged him to be courageous and resilient. So as his curiosity about animals grew, he asked me what the *bravest* animal was. That's when I introduced him to the honey badger.

If you've never seen one in action, do yourself a favor and look it up—there's a famous video of a honey badger taking on an entire pack of lions. Pound for pound, it's one of the most fearless creatures on the planet.

Today, my son loves and sleeps with a honey badger stuffed animal he named Gritty—a nod to one of our family values. (Shout-out to Bill High and the workshop where my wife and I first named the core values we want to instill in our family: God, grit, gratitude, and generosity.) His teacher even sketched a honey badger for him that now hangs, framed, on his bedroom wall. Ask him what his favorite color is, he'll tell you, "Black and white, like a honey badger."

Now, would it be wise for my son to literally charge into battle with a pack of lions? Of course not, outside of the unlikely event that he ends up in a pickle like the prophet Daniel's. But I *do* want him to carry that same fearless posture when life presents him with choices—when the path forward demands courage, when fear whispers one thing and faith calls for another.

That same posture—brave but not reckless—is the foundation of stewardship as a way of life.

Because when it comes to money, we're often presented with two extremes: play it safe out of fear or live recklessly out of impulse. But biblical stewardship charts a different course. It's bold *and* wise. It's grounded in faith, not fear, but anchored in discipline, not impulse. It's about stepping into a different way of handling money, one that requires courage, yes, but also wisdom, patience, and purpose. It's taking some wise risks, in faith, instead of hoarding and spending out of selfishness and fear.

And just like the honey badger, it means not backing down from hard decisions. It means living intentionally, not reactively. It means choosing to live by faith, even when fear is the easier option.

Our courage is founded on the knowledge that God owns it all. If we strive to make wise, loving choices with the good gifts he's given us, we can trust him to guide us in those steps. That attitude of stewardship, that way of life, can shape our daily decisions and set the stage for how we approach money and how we spend, save, and give.

Focus Questions

1. When you think about success, what comes to mind first—possessions, status, security, appearance, or something else? How aligned is your current view with God's definition of stewardship?
2. What kind of financial margin (or lack of it) exists in your life right now? How does that margin (or the absence of it) impact your peace, your time, and your ability to serve others?
3. Are there any areas of your life—your money, your time, your gifts—where you're acting more like an owner than a steward? What would it look like to surrender those back to God?

Do It Today

Take fifteen to thirty minutes today to do a simple stewardship inventory.

Divide a piece of paper into six columns labeled: **Money • Time/ Energy • Talents • Stuff • Relationships • Body**

In each column, jot down how you're currently using those resources. Then ask:

* Am I using this to serve myself or others?
* Am I managing this resource as if it belongs to God?

Circle one small area in each column where you could make a shift toward more intentional, God-honoring stewardship this week. Then pray and commit it to him.

Part 2

THE FOUNDATIONS

Chapter 3

PLAY YOUR OWN GAME

Each one should test their own actions. Then they can take
pride in themselves alone, without comparing themselves to
someone else, for each one should carry their own load.

—GALATIANS 6:4–5

THE SOCIAL MEDIA HIGHLIGHT REEL

Comparison is no longer just a natural human instinct. Thanks to social media, it's been twisted and upped by a factor of about a thousand.

We no longer stop at comparing ourselves with our direct neighbors; we keep going, and we measure ourselves against every influencer and random connection whose polished lives we can see on display online. Our brains go floating off into the ether of someone else's curated, perfect social media life, and we are so, so tempted to play someone else's game instead of our own: instead of the one God has called each of us, with our unique contexts and God-given gifts, to play.

Have you heard the saying "Whoever dies with the most toys wins"? What an awful sentiment. But the reality is we tend to see financial success as a scorecard. I know I'm guilty of this; I used to habitually look up trends around net worth by age, trying to make sure I was in a nice upper bracket. I also remember my mother watching The Suze Orman show. Did she watch it to learn a thing or two about finances? Yes, but I believe it was *more* about seeing how she measured up to her pre-retiree peers who were calling and writing in.

We want nice homes and clothes and vacations, and we want to post them on our profiles so other people will know we're thriving. Over time, as we live into that hunger, our very perception of the world changes. Our ears perk up at the sound of loose change and the ping of a "like" instead of at the sound of a bird song or a loved one's real, in-person voice.

We need to cut it out. You aren't going to keep up with the Joneses because the Joneses aren't real. Those lives you see on your screen? They are carefully polished and served up for your personal displeasure. Ignore them. Play your own game.

Shiny social media highlight reels have made it all much worse, but the comparison trap is nothing new. If you really want to understand how powerful the pull of comparison can be, just ask someone who lived through the great "Tickle Me Elmo" craze of the mid-'90s.[8] But if you talk to a parent of a preschooler from that era, be kind: you might trigger some deeply buried Christmas season trauma.

In July of '96, a toy company called Tyco released Tickle Me Elmo, a red, fuzzy stuffed animal version of the beloved Sesame Street character. Elmo would laugh and shake when you squeezed him three times, which was, of course, adorable, but nothing to get worked up about, right? But then Rosie O'Donnell—basically the '90s version of Ellen—gave away two hundred Elmos on her show in October, and suddenly, Elmo became the must-have toy of the year.

It spiraled so quickly after that. Stores couldn't keep them on shelves. Fights broke out. Shoppers were literally trampled. Elmos were resold for over $1,000 each. Meanwhile, little preschoolers across America were issuing ultimatums: "Elmo or bust, Mom."

Now, imagine that same frenzy in today's world, but with social media magnifying it and *really* sending things through the roof.

Let's picture a mom who manages to snag a coveted Elmo for her child and proudly posts a photo on Instagram, captioned something like "Christmas came early for our little one." All her "friends" see it—including another mom of a preschooler who hasn't been able to find one. Cue the instant wave of jealousy and self-doubt. *Why didn't I try harder? Am I a bad mom?*

But it doesn't stop there. The Elmo-holding mom also happens to be posting from their Thanksgiving family trip—in New York City—where they're planning to attend the Macy's Thanksgiving Day Parade. Meanwhile, the mom scrolling through this post is sitting on the couch while her husband is watching football, and now she's not just comparing toys—she's comparing vacations, marriages, parenting, and life choices.

And just for good measure, she's not the only one seeing the post. Multiply that moment of discontent by fifty other moms who saw the same cutesy photo and caption, many of whom the original poster hasn't even seen or talked to in years. Maybe they just went to high school together. Maybe they live in completely different states now. But thanks to one accepted friend request and an algorithm that loves to stir the pot, the comparison game is alive and well.

That's the world we live in. The Tickle Me Elmo chaos was real—but in the social media era, comparison isn't just a moment in a toy aisle. It's a constant stream of highlights, filters, and subtle reminders that we're always a few steps behind someone else's (maybe not as perfect as it looks, but that doesn't make you feel any better, does it?) life.

There's a word for this exhausting byproduct of comparison: FOMO—the fear of missing out.

FOMO AND FOBO: THE MODERN COMPARISON TRAP

FOMO's a relatively new term, but its impact has been felt throughout human history. It's really just a new way of describing that drive to keep up with the Joneses as we talked about above, but I'd say it's even something a little bit more than that. It's not just that we want to *be* like the people around us. It's that we don't want to miss out on *anything* our neighbors have or experience because we're hungry for something good. "Maybe *that*," we tell ourselves as we look at someone else's car, home, clothes, or life, "is what would fill me up. I'll never know till I get it. So I'd better get it, or else I'll never know if I've missed out on the best thing ever."

On top of that fear of missing out, we're also pulled to measure our own worth—and the deep worth of others—by what we *have*. In 1954, psychologist Leon Festiger proposed that humans have an inherent drive to compare themselves with others, which can lead to feelings of inadequacy when others seem to have better experiences or possessions.[9] Festiger called this concept the social comparison theory. Years later, we saw this concept become more pervasive as marketers began using the phrase "limited time only" in their product ads to create a sense of urgency around consumer products. Quick, get it now, or you'll be the only person you know who doesn't have a Tickle Me Elmo, and won't that be *deeply embarrassing*?

Nowadays, we've also got FOBO going around—a fear of better options. This is what happens when we're inundated with possibilities. The world of social media shows us not just the job, the home, the lifestyle that's in front of us, but the whole range of potential human possessions and experiences. We see what everyone around us has. Then we see what's being offered to us. If we perceive there's a gap between what *they* have and what's available to us right now, we might be tempted to avoid making a decision, to wait until something better comes along. It's just FOMO with different clothes on, but instead of making us run around madly grabbing at the toys we think we need to feel successful, it makes us freeze. We've been offered a job, a college scholarship, a relationship, the chance to travel, but we wonder if a better job, college, girlfriend, or trip might be out there. We don't want to limit ourselves and miss out on that one thing that may fill us up, convince us we're as good as everyone else. So we wait a little longer. And as we wait, envying everyone around us and telling ourselves that our turn will come any day, it all passes us by.

We can see both FOMO and FOBO, these twin sides of the same comparison trap, play out in the lives of high schoolers and college students especially. (No judgment: we've all been there.) At this stage, young people are feeling the pressure to grow up, to become more independent, and are trying to find themselves. This makes them particularly vulnerable to comparison. Seeing their peers' academic, athletic, and relationship highlight reels on social media leaves many confusing their social worth with their self-worth. Whether it's FOMO that has them grasping at everything they see or FOBO that gets them hesitating and holding back for that "just right" thing, they're basing who they are, their value as human beings, on what the people around them are doing and getting and posting proudly on the feeds.

Does that sound like someone you know? Trying to keep up with your peers' near-perfect social media persona, the one that is so carefully curated to incite feelings of jealousy, envy, and praise, will not only lead to poor mental and emotional conditions like anxiety, depression, and isolation; it can also produce potentially destructive physical and financial habits.

POOR SPENDING, INSTANT GRATIFICATION: THE CONSEQUENCES OF FOMO

The harmful physical habits formed by comparison have been well documented: young people, in particular, are tempted to over-exercise or under-eat in order to look a certain way. And while the physical responses are generally more catastrophically harmful, the money habits formed during this time can also wreak havoc on a young person's financial health.

Comparison triggers consumption, and impulse leads to debt. Allow me to explain how this could play out.

Let's say you're on social media and you see a picture of the most popular guy at school having lunch with three of your school's prettiest girls. Big smiles all around and they're each enjoying a nice burrito bowl at Chipotle. You're immediately hungry, so you click the hashtag #ChipotleLidFlip (yeah, apparently that's a thing?), and it takes you to Chipotle's site for quick ordering. You're sulking in your jammies and don't really want to leave the house, so you pay the extra delivery fees and tip for DoorDash to deliver.

Now, back to the picture. Mr. Joe Cool has some nice drip too. That shirt he's wearing? For your convenience (and envy), he's graciously hashtagged the brand name for you in the comments. You click on the link and find the shirt.

You've never ordered that brand because it's very expensive, so you don't know what size to pick. The size chart recommends you buy an extra-large. You click on XL, and guess what? Out of stock. You immediately feel body shame and Chipotle burrito bowl buyer's remorse, so you click on a size smaller. A button pops up asking you if you want to buy now.

Once you click Buy Now, you realize you don't have enough money in your checking account to make the purchase. But to your delight, ApplePay, where your credit card is linked, is available. You jump all over it with just one click.

Do you see the dangerous, slippery slope of comparison? That one post by someone who had everything you thought you wanted in that snapshot of time led you down a path of envy, which ultimately led to two impulse buys in less than five minutes. It's a sick dopamine cycle that led you to overspending, and if you do that every day: boom, lifestyle creep. Anyway, was it at all worth it? No, really, was it?

> **Lifestyle Creep:** When you make a little more, so you spend a little more. Then you make a little more, and spend a little more—on and on till you're living a far more lavish lifestyle than makes sense.

You felt bad about your weight after being compelled to go down a size, so you threw the burrito bowl in the trash when DoorDash delivered it and told yourself you were going to lose ten pounds in order for the shirt to fit. For convenience of delivery, you spent thirty dollars for a ten-dollar burrito bowl you didn't end up eating. A burrito bowl that wasn't even in your mind before seeing the post. The hundred-dollar shirt that's currently too small for you actually cost you $110 because you paid the minimum required each month on your credit card and let interest compound to your detriment (more on that in a later chapter). What's tragic is not just the wasted burrito bowl, the undersized shirt—it's the wasted peace, the wasted money, the wasted contentment.

So next time you see Mr. Joe Cool flaunting his drip and bussin' food, don't let it make you delulu, just consider his perceived rizz to be sus. (How's that for some young people lingo?)

In all seriousness, though, don't fall into the FOMO trap. Remember the often-shared phrase "Comparison is the thief of joy"? The quote is attributed to President Theodore Roosevelt, and I believe those words to be true. But I also believe that comparison not only steals our joy but also robs us of a bright financial future by tempting us to spend money on things that don't matter, just so we can feel adequate or validated.

WHO ARE WE TRYING TO IMPRESS?

Does any of this sound like you? If so, I want to take a minute to remind you that your worth doesn't come from what others think or say about you or even what you think or say about yourself. Your worth comes from what Jesus says about you. You are a child of God. He made you, and you are wonderfully made. You don't have to look further than the Bible for confirmation of this:

- *"Behold what manner of love the Father has bestowed on us, that we should be called children of God!"* (1 John 3:1 NKJV)
- *"So God created man in His own image; in the image of God He created him; male and female He created them."* (Genesis 1:27 ESV)
- *"For you formed my inward parts; you knitted me together in my mother's womb. I praise you, for I am fearfully and wonderfully made. Wonderful are your works; my soul knows it very well."* (Psalm 139:13–14 ESV)

Success isn't about public applause. It's about resting in your identity in Christ and stewarding well *whatever* you have been given. Financial success, with all its trappings, is a false scorecard.

Are you in a good situation, money-wise? Don't fall into the comparison trap. Be humble, watch out for pride, practice gratitude, and level up your generosity by giving more money and time. You're probably an ambitious person—so use that ambition for *good*.

Are you in a rough financial spot? Don't you fall into the comparison trap either: don't let your temporary money struggles define you. Take an honest assessment of where money is going and cut wherever necessary. Identify areas where God has uniquely gifted you (he's given all of us gifts) and find ways to earn money by using those gifts. Seek wise counsel and mentors, keep a positive attitude, and choose to be a victor, not a victim.

Proverbs 30:8–9 says, *"First, help me never to tell a lie. Second, give me neither poverty nor riches. Give me just enough to satisfy my needs. For if I grow rich, I may deny you and say, 'Who is the LORD?' And if I am too poor, I may steal and thus insult God's holy name."* Don't aim to be a rich punk *or* a poor thief. Aim simply to be wise, trusting in God to care for your needs while living generously, less worried about how you compare to others than how much good you can do with the limited time and funds you have. Maybe you'll end up somewhere in that big middle space between "rich punk" and "poor thief," but you will be living a life that is anything but average. I once heard someone say, "The real measure of your wealth is how much you'd be worth if you lost all your money."[10] I know for sure that's how God sees it.

So quit the comparison trap. Choose contentment and gratitude over consumerism. Bloom where you're planted, and steward every good gift from God without worrying too much about what others are doing.

Focus Questions

1. What areas of your life are most vulnerable to comparison? Is it your finances, your appearance, your career path, your relationships?
2. Who are your "Joneses"? Who do you most often compare yourself to, either online or in real life? What effect does that have on your mindset?
3. What kinds of posts or people tend to trigger FOMO or FOBO in you? Why do you think that is?
4. What are three unique strengths or blessings God has given *you* that are worth celebrating without comparing?

Do It Today

Start a "Gratitude over Comparison" list.

Open a fresh note on your phone or in your journal and write down ten things you're grateful for that have *nothing* to do with what *other people* have or think.

Examples include the following:

- "I made a friend laugh today."
- "I have warm socks."
- "God is faithful."

Whenever comparison creeps in, go back and add to the list.

Chapter 4

DON'T WASTE YOUR TALENTS

*The place God calls you to is the place where your deep
gladness and the world's deep hunger meet.*

—FREDERICK BUECHNER

STEWARDING YOUR TALENTS

Everything you have is on loan from God.

Yes, I know you've heard me say that already. I know we've already gone over the concept of stewardship in detail, but I can't emphasize this mind-blowing reality enough.

If you're like most people I know, you've probably grown up being blasted with a certain kind of message about the pattern your life is supposed to follow. Get good grades, get into a good college, get a good career, live a good life. But what does all that "good" actually look like? Is all this talk about a "good" career just about finding work that just pays the bills? Is it about finding a way to build yourself an indulgently comfortable life? Is it still a "good" career even if you barely have time to see your spouse or kids every day, even if you're inadvertently padding the pockets of an exploitative leader or system, even if your work doesn't do any tangible good for anyone in the end?

Of course not. We get this one life. We're given our few talents. We're not meant to blow it on anything less than service to others and the furthering of God's kingdom and glory. *That's it.* Work that is truly good is the work God wants you doing. And he equips you to do that work with some skills and talents that are uniquely yours. He expects you to use your gifts for good. The end.

What a crazy truth. And it's one that is absolutely essential to grasp before you can hope to ever truly handle money God's way, stepping into career and financial decisions with that faithful stewardship mindset. It will *change your life* when you understand and accept that God hasn't just charged you with using your money, time, and possessions for good. He expects you to steward your gifts and strengths, your intelligence, your passions and dreams and emotions too. Your very heart, mind, and soul belong to God: and he is calling you to use them well, like the precious, borrowed things they are. You're the manager, not the owner, and it's your task to work with *intention* rather than *self-indulgence*. What you do every day? It matters. You have to believe that in order to step whole-heartedly into a life spent using your gifts and talents for God's glory, in service of those around you.

But what, specifically, does that mean for *you*? How can you know what your unique talents really are? And once you identify them, then how are you supposed to determine where and how God is calling you to put them to good use?

Well, that's between you and God to work out in the end. But here are a few tips on getting started.

WHAT ARE MY TALENTS?

Did you grow up watching Veggie Tales? Or am I dating myself by even referencing good old Bob the tomato and Larry the cucumber?

If you have no idea what I'm talking about, my apologies. For those of you who *have* seen Veggie Tales, though, I wonder if you recognize this line: "God made you special, and he loves you very much. Bye."

Every episode of the classic Veggie Tales stories ended with that message, and it's a statement that gets in your head, especially when you're a little kid watching your favorite crunchy green characters sing goofy songs on repeat. In between the giggles, you hear a familiar voice reminding you: You were specially, lovingly created to be *uniquely you*. Talking vegetable aside, what a powerful statement that is.

But what does it really mean that God "made us special"? Sure, he purposely gifted us each our own particular strengths and abilities, but just saying that is so much easier than actually identifying *how* God created us uniquely. It can be a lifelong challenge to nail down exactly which talents God specifically chose to entrust us with and how we're meant to use them.

Maybe you're trying to choose a college major. Maybe you're contemplating your long-term career with real seriousness for the first time because you know you're called to be God's hands and feet in this world, and you want to be where he wants you, doing the good work he wants you doing. Whatever the case, if you're at a moment in your life where you're mulling over what gifts God has given you so you know how to steward them well and use them for his glory, take a moment to reflect on these questions:

- What makes you unique?
- What lights you up?
- What comes easy to you?
- When do you find yourself experiencing "flow"—really getting in the zone and moving with natural confidence?

Your answers to these questions are crucial. Dig into them as your starting point. Ask close loved ones their thoughts, if you like, but listen to that quiet voice inside most intently.

Then, don't stop there. This question has to do with way more than what you can find just by looking inward. God is at work in the world around you every day, and chances are he wants you to join him in whatever he's up to. Look outward: at your neighborhood, your church, your city, your country, the world. Where's the need? Where's the opportunity? As Frederick Buechner put it in the quote opening this chapter, your calling has something to do with the intersection between your own deep-rooted passions and skills and the hungers and needs of the people and creation around you.

Calling: God's direction for your life: the path he desires **you specifically** to follow so you can best bear his image, serve others, and honor him in everything you are and everything you do.

Once you identify your talents and compare them against where God is at work and calling you to join him, you might start to question whether your talents are suited to the task. You might feel like the gifts you have are inadequate or ill-matched for the challenge God is drawing you toward. Maybe you're shocked to find God isn't calling you to use that skill that comes easy after all, but instead is asking you to work in a way that *doesn't* come so easy—though most likely it's something you know you could manage, and manage well, with a little extra effort. That's life.

Though it's a good first step to identify your natural, easy-flowing gifts, the surprising truth is that the easiest option ain't always the best one. Finding yourself called to a hard path can be daunting, but I find reassurance in the fact that there are *so* many examples in the Bible of God pulling a person into a difficult task, then equipping them for the challenge along the way, once they've moved into the work with faith. Some of God's gifts are ones you're born with; others, he likes to give you a hand in cultivating later.

Personally, I've always had a head for numbers and finances; part of what drew me to my line of work was my personal interest, which, combined with some natural skill, grew to a passion. As I advanced in my career, I also advanced in my earnings until, eventually, I reached a point where I was so financially comfortable that money itself no longer had the power to push me to even greater heights. I was earning more than enough, so I got complacent. And once I got complacent, I started to wonder: "Outside of providing the money my family needs, what is all this work I do really *for*?"

I had to shift my mindset. No longer driven by the narrative "I need to earn enough for my family," I was finally able to assess how misaligned my motives were and to pivot so that I was functioning from a narrative of stewardship. I turned my eyes toward my clients, developed a genuine heart for service, and was never happier. I'd been using my God-given skills all along, but it wasn't until I finally turned my eyes outward that I used them the right way. Around the same time, I started doing work with some friends with special needs. Now, that's not necessarily work that comes naturally and easily to me, but I felt God's pull, so I put in the effort to cultivate my attitude and skills to that end. The more deeply I engaged in that volunteer work, the more I understood that how we spend our days *matters*, whether we're using the skills that come easy to us or the ones that take work, whether we're earning actual money or not.

This section isn't meant to provide you with a clear guide for choosing your career and life's path, but I do want to stress that clarifying what your gifts are and how you can nurture and use them for service is a crucial first step to learning to steward them well. If you want to dig deeper into tools for identifying your talents, there are a plethora of tests out there that can tell you more about your strengths and weaknesses, your spiritual gifts, and your personality.

Personally, I highly recommend checking out Max Lucado's book, *Cure for the Common Life: Living in Your Sweet Spot.* He lays out a truly powerful framework, the STORY method, for identifying that "sweet spot" where your unique strengths can be used for God's glory in your everyday life. The book was a game-changer for me, and I'm sure it could be for you as well.

THE INFINITE GAME: A CAUTION AGAINST THE FIRE MOVEMENT (AND YOLO LIVING)

Now that we've spent some time really digging into the importance of stewarding our gifts, skills, and talents, I wanted to direct a word at all the ambitious overachievers out there. You're the ones who are willing to really put your nose to the grindstone when you have a reward in your sights. You're the ones who didn't fail the marshmallow test.

Haven't heard of the marshmallow test? In the 1960s, Stanford researchers conducted a study on delayed gratification.[11] Children were given one marshmallow and told that if they could wait fifteen minutes without eating it, they'd receive a second one. Unsurprisingly, a lot of those tykes just couldn't grasp the concept of waiting: *Gulp!* Down went marshmallow number one, even though they'd been warned there'd be no number two without patience. Follow-up studies found that the kids who *did* wait long enough to earn a second marshmallow tended to achieve more in school, experience less stress, and enjoy better life outcomes overall. The ability to delay gratification is powerful—but like any strength, it can become a weakness if it's used in the wrong way, for the wrong ends.

Let's take a look at the FIRE movement: financial independence, retire early. On the surface, it sounds like a dream. If you live well below your means and save like crazy, you can retire by forty and live the rest of your life in sweet, comfortable freedom. For a driven, goal-oriented person, that's an appealing goal. In fact, when I was in my twenties, I remember telling people I wanted to retire by thirty. That was long before FIRE was a thing, but I was surrounded by people who treated retirement as life's final goalpost, so I ran toward it with everything I had, intent on capturing the proverbial flag.

> **The FIRE Movement:** A lifestyle and financial philosophy focused on aggressively saving and investing in order to achieve financial independence and retire as early as humanly possible.

But here's the thing. Retirement is not, should not be, the ultimate goal. It's not in God's design at all. As we've just discussed above, our true ultimate goal ought to have a little something to do with diligent service to others and God. Chasing a quick end to the "drudgery" of work in order to do "whatever you want" for the rest of your days? I get the appeal. But that's the opposite of what we're called to do.

As I shared before, I eventually came to see my work not as a means to an end but as a way to serve others. I started to enjoy my work more. I wasn't chasing money so that I could retire young. I was pursuing purpose because I had a gift that I could use to help people, and helping people was something I could do for the rest of my life. I realized I had been treating life like a finite game—one with set rules, a clear endpoint, and a winner. As Simon Sinek explores in *The Infinite Game*, some games never *really* end. Your life is constantly evolving, and although your endpoint is technically death, you have no way of knowing when the buzzer for your game of life will sound. With infinite games, you succeed by continuing to play and adapt. The goal isn't to "win" but to *stay in the game* and *keep playing it well.*

Think about it: if we are called to work well and use our gifts for God's glory, what could be more self-defeating than focusing on ending your time of useful employment as soon as possible?

But wait, can you live with an infinite mindset in a career that has a defined retirement age? Say you're a teacher employed by the state. You're guaranteed a comfy retirement after a set number of years of service, and that sounds pretty great to you. You can't possibly see yourself dealing with snotty-nosed elementary school kids past your "finite" years of service. You're imagining that recently retired coworker of yours who now spends her days playing pickleball and tending to her garden. Now *that's* the life, you say.

But is it really? I'm not saying that teacher ought to refuse to retire. I'm saying she could refuse to quit her calling. Even if we eventually stop working in one form, we don't have to stop stewarding our gifts and showing up with purpose.

It reminds me of John Piper's take on a *Reader's Digest* article that he referenced in his book *Don't Waste Your Life*. Piper writes:

> *I will tell you what a tragedy is. I will show you how to waste your life. Consider a story from the February 1998 edition of **Reader's Digest**, which tells about a couple who 'took early retirement from their jobs in the Northeast five years ago when he was fifty-nine and she was fifty-one. Now they live in Punta Gorda, Florida, where they cruise on their 30-foot trawler, play softball, and collect shells.'*

At first, when I read it I thought it might be a joke. A spoof on the American Dream. But it wasn't. Tragically, this was the dream: Come to the end of your life—your one and only precious, God-given life—and let the last great work of your life, before you give an account to your Creator, be this: playing softball and collecting shells.

Picture them before Christ at the great day of judgment: "Look, Lord. See my shells." That is a tragedy. And people today are spending billions of dollars to persuade you to embrace that tragic dream. Over against that, I put my protest: Don't buy it. Don't waste your life.[12]

I've experienced this firsthand. After years of helping clients prepare for "comfortable retirement," I had the chance to sell my business and take a step back. It seemed ideal—more time for my family, my hobbies, and some well-earned rest. But almost immediately, I realized comfort wasn't what I truly needed. A life of relaxation and "doing whatever I want" was *not* what I was created for.

Jesus tells the story of the rich fool in Luke 12, the man who stored up more than enough and then said to himself, "Take it easy. Eat, drink, and be merry." But God calls him a fool: "Tonight your life will be demanded from you." The problem wasn't the man's wealth. It was that he filled his barns with self and not with God.

You're going to get sick of hearing me say it, but stewardship isn't just about how we use our money. It's also about how we use our talents. Your gifts were given for a purpose far greater than personal success or early retirement. Don't bury them. Don't waste them. Don't end the game early.

The world keeps trying to sell you a self-centered dream. FIRE glorifies long-term comfort. There's also the YOLO mindset ("You only live once, so make the most of each moment.") which glorifies short-term pleasure. Both have some value, I suppose—FIRE teaches discipline and planning; YOLO encourages presence, creativity, and boldness—but both fall short when they leave God out of the picture. The former will give you a long life of comfort and ease, but to what end? And the latter can propel you into long-term regret over your recklessness, bad decisions, and lack of planning.

You were made for more than selfish comfort or day-to-day thrills. You were made for a purpose.

Keep showing up. Keep serving. Stay in the game.

REGRET AND DECISION-MAKING

When I say that God calls us to steward our talents well, I mean that he wants us to be wise, intentional, and selfless in how we use them. Whether we like it or not, that requires forethought and planning. I mentioned that the long-term consequence of living with a YOLO mindset can be regret: regret over reckless decisions and over a lack of planning. Sure, we aren't meant to micromanage our own lives (they aren't ours, after all) or to get too rigid and focused on achieving our own worldly success, as discussed above, but wise stewardship generally isn't something we can just jump into daily, going off the cuff, either. A jumble of days spent like that adds up to what, exactly?

To steward your talents well, you need to engage in purposeful, long-term planning and decision-making in order to avoid deep-rooted *regret*.

Here's a thought exercise: Imagine yourself at ninety. Given where you see your life going at this point in time, what do you suspect you'll wish you'd done differently once you find yourself at the end? Really let yourself picture it; I know it can be tough. The first time I asked myself this question and really let myself get inside the mind of a ninety-year-old me, it felt like a punch to the gut. We all like to think we're living in a way that is meaningful, faithful, and good, but poke your head up out of the busyness of the day-to-day, look backward and forward, and chances are you'll see a big change or two just begging to be made.

Palliative care nurse Bronnie Ware wrote a whole book exploring the top five regrets she heard expressed by her patients as they approached their final days:[13]

- ◆ Regret over living the life others expected them to live instead of the life they truly longed for or felt called toward

- Regret over working too hard, chasing paychecks instead of spending time with family
- Regret over not courageously expressing their feelings when it mattered
- Regret over losing touch with friends they cared about deeply, failing to maintain valuable relationships simply because life got full and busy
- Regret over not choosing to be content and find their own joy, whatever the circumstances

Take a moment to reflect on those regrets. Do any of them hit a nerve?

When I look at them all together like that, I see evidence of the human longing for a deeply meaningful life. That's what we all really want, isn't it? And we can only achieve it through service, stewardship, plus a dose of wisdom and big-picture decision-making.

By the way, when it comes to the practical process of decision-making, I find the 10-10-10 framework from Suzy Welch to be super helpful:[14]

- Ten minutes from now, how will I feel about this decision?
- Ten months from now, how will I feel about this decision?
- Ten years from now, how will I feel about this decision?

Your talents are worth investing well, and God calls you to use them as best you can for his kingdom. Give it your best effort by planning wisely and making your daily and long-term decisions with thoughtful intentionality.

WASTED TIME, WASTED EFFORT

OK, say you've identified your gifts, prayerfully considered how God wants you to use them to serve others, and engaged in wise decision-making to move forward. You're trying your best to steward your gifts and talents in a way that serves others, but chances are things won't go *exactly* to plan. You get a job, and *maybe* it's the job you know you're called to stay in long-term, that aligns with passions and values and God's calling for your life; but maybe, in your mind at least, it's more of a pit stop along the way toward what you believe to be your larger purpose.

Maybe that difference affects how you treat it. Maybe the diligence and effort you put into the work and the rest of your life varies based on whether you think you've found "your thing" or are just still existing and hopefully on your way to "your thing" someday soon. If the job sucks, you aren't paid enough and your boss is a jerk—well, that sure makes it all the harder to give a flip.

But guess what? Whether you're just working at a coffee shop or have settled into a career as outwardly meaningful as ministry, social services, or medical work: God expects you to steward the days of life that he graciously gifted you with the *same level* of care and intentionality. What you do with your time and talent matters just as much, whether you're serving orphans, fighting fires, taking orders, or punching numbers.

Talking about this always makes me think of my parents. My dad worked up on a roof all day and came home with the smell of sawdust on him—goodness, I came to love that smell. Then, even after a long day of work, he'd take me outside to practice baseball or basketball. And my mom? She got up early to go sort mail at the post office. It wasn't a job that paid the big bucks, and she still came home from that early shift to cook supper, clean the house, and do the laundry before Dad and us kids came back for the day. I am positive neither of them would say they were working their "dream jobs," but you know what? They gave it their all, and they took real pride in their work. To this day, even though they've since retired, I still run into people who share memories and compliments about my parents' work.

Whether you're currently working in your ideal job or not, give it your best. Martin Luther King Jr. once said, "If a man is called to be a street sweeper, he should sweep streets even as a Michaelangelo painted, or Beethoven composed music or Shakespeare wrote poetry. He should sweep streets so well that all the hosts of heaven and earth will pause to say, 'Here lived a great street sweeper who did his job well.'"[15]

No matter what you do, you have the opportunity to improve the world for those around you. Think about your experience grabbing lunch at Chick-fil-A versus, say, McDonald's. A little positivity and diligence go a long way, and hey, if people notice it and that leads to some future opportunities, that's a handy little byproduct.

One way we can make sure we're giving our work our all? Good time management.

TIME MANAGEMENT

Whether you pour all your effort and best intentions into each day or just float through it with a meh attitude, there's always a risk that you'll waste your time thanks to distractions or habits that lead to general ineffectiveness. And your time, just as much as your talents, is another resource we're called to steward well.

There are some kind of hilarious, kind of depressing stats out there about the time-wasting that happens at work these days. Studies show that employees check their emails up to 121 times a day and spend 7.5 hours a week browsing social media *during work hours.*[16] And it's not just at work, of course. How much time do you spend on your couch, zoning out on your phone or Netflix, when you know you'll be kicking yourself later for not doing that workout, calling that friend, working on that hobby, reading that book?

Thanks to the constant distractions of our portable entertainment devices, it's easier now than ever to waste time—and that's alarming when we remember that it isn't really *our* time at all. It's God's. When we give in to the distractions all around us, choosing mindless relaxation over things that actually matter and activities that make a difference, *we are wasting God's time.*

I want to drop a note here that, of course, there's a difference between time-wasting laziness and much-needed rest. God created the Sabbath, after all. Psalm 127:2 tells us, *"In vain you rise early and stay up late, toiling for food to eat—for he grants sleep to those he loves."* Getting roped into workaholism and hustle culture is a negative, for sure. I'm just saying that apathy and sloth are too.

Proverbs 6 gives us the flip side of that coin: *"A little sleep, a little slumber, a little folding of the hands to rest—and poverty will come on you like a thief and scarcity like an armed man."* There's a difference between healthy rhythms of work and rest and the endemic patterns of time-wasting that are so pervasive in today's world.

I'm talking a lot about this one, but for a clearcut description of that need for diligence, regardless of circumstances, you don't need to look any further than Scripture:

> *Servants, do what you're told by your earthly masters. And don't just do the minimum that will get you by. Do your best. Work from the heart for your real Master, for God, confident that you'll get paid in full when you come into your inheritance. Keep in mind always that the ultimate Master you're serving is Christ. The sullen servant who does shoddy work will be held responsible. Being a follower of Jesus doesn't cover up bad work.* (Colossians 3:22–25 MSG)

There's one example of good hard work and diligence. First Corinthians 10:31 provides another: *"So whether you eat or drink or whatever you do, do it all for the glory of God."*

So, we need to manage our time well so we can steward our talents well and make a positive impact on the world around us. That's easier said than done in our distraction-packed society, so I wanted to share some of my top tips and resources to support you in the journey:

* Need help prioritizing your tasks? Check out the Eisenhower matrix.[17] You take all your tasks and categorize them into quadrants based on urgency and importance, and the visual organization it provides is truly transformative. It can be a big help for sussing out sneaky distractions and time-wasters, too.

Eisenhower Matrix

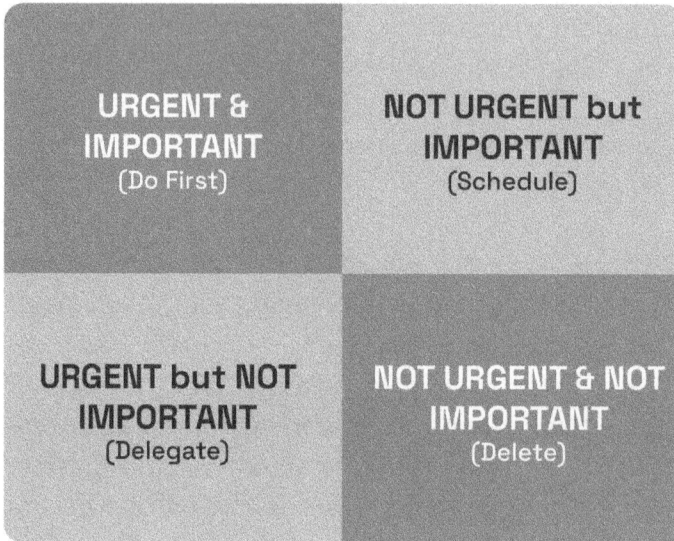

URGENT & IMPORTANT (Do First)	NOT URGENT but IMPORTANT (Schedule)
URGENT but NOT IMPORTANT (Delegate)	NOT URGENT & NOT IMPORTANT (Delete)

- I'll bet you've heard of SMART goals. Specific, measurable, achievable, relevant, and time-bound goals make all the difference for time management, really and truly: try it out.
- Another tip: create daily habits and build on them. I'm talking about habit stacking, specifically as James Clear describes the process.[18] The basic idea is this: you choose an existing habit you have and glue another good habit to it. When you engage in the existing habit (say, having your morning cup of coffee), you also engage in the new habit: directly before, directly after, or even during (say, tidying one area of your house, doing a certain exercise, or reading your Bible).
- Clear also speaks specifically about the power of an identity shift: telling yourself you're the kind of person who does whatever it is you want to be doing. For example, for me, once I started telling myself, "I'm a healthy person," I found it much easier to get up at 5:00 a.m. to work out, which led to better eating (because if I make the sacrifice of getting up early and working out, I'm not going to throw away my progress by eating like crap). And the same thing can happen with money and stewardship: saying

"I'm a hard worker" or "I make wise money choices" can make a huge difference.

A WORD ABOUT WHERE YOU WORK

At the time of this writing, in the aftermath of the COVID-19 pandemic, hybrid and work-from-home employment have become increasingly, the norm. That can be great, especially for parents with young kids. But there's a good chance, if you're reading this book, that you are *not* a parent with young kids. You're probably a young adult just starting out in your career, and learning what it means to steward your time and talents *now* should take precedence.

So here's my two cents: if you're a young person with no kids, and *especially* if you live alone, working from home is almost always a poor choice. It leads to isolation—you're sacrificing the networking, mentors, and relationships that only come with working alongside actual people in real time and in real life. Working from home can lead to anxiety, disconnection from and discontentment with the work, and it can draw you into seeking out negative sources for happiness and fulfillment, from retail therapy to online gambling (both just a click away from your Teams meeting or spreadsheet).

I have been blown away, in recent years, by Gen Z's firm insistence that they get what they need and earn what they're worth at their jobs, including remote employment options whenever possible. On the one hand, I applaud them. Man, the courage of some of these young employees. The age-old norms of keeping your head down, putting in overtime without complaint? They're on their way out, and in so many ways, that's a good thing.

On the other hand, there's a fine line between fighting to adjust a toxic corporate culture and settling down a bit too firmly into a focus on your own rights and desires until it morphs into *entitlement.* Do you really *need* to work from home, with the ability to wear pajama bottoms and snack all day? Would the slightly less comfortable option of getting your hands a little dirty, dealing with messy humans in real life, and doing work in an environment where other real people are also working and building something good together really be that bad?

Here's a statement I want you to take to heart, not just on the work-from-home/return-to-office issue. *Choose the hard path.* It's often the best one, no matter what you're told by this society that is so abundant with ease and comfort right now. An easy, comfortable life is not God's design for you or for anyone. We were not created to sleepwalk through life, talking to zero people face-to-face each day and sipping our endless iced coffees from the couch. We were created to *live*.

YOUR AUDIENCE OF ONE

In the end, if you step into this stewardship thought process and strive to do the best you can with the talents and skills you've been given, remember: it's not ultimately for applause from your boss, likes on social media, or even the approval of family. It's for your audience of one. Work like God is watching because he is. Not from a distance, but up close and personal. He sees every effort, every moment you choose integrity, every time you show up faithfully, even when no one else notices. Be thankful for the gifts he's given you, no matter how unimpressive you may think they are. If you gave someone a gift and they gave you a stank face back, you'd want to snatch the gift away, wouldn't you? Now imagine how God feels when we complain about our abilities, compare them to others, or bury them out of fear or pride.

The best way to show gratitude is to use your talents—for service, for growth, and for God's glory. That's stewardship. It might mean investing in yourself through things like coaching and credentialing programs, not for ego, but so you can better bless others. Think of the athlete who coasted on raw talent but was never pushed to grow, who eventually plateaued. Or the dentist who stopped learning, refused to figure out new technologies, and lost his edge. Gifts that aren't stewarded well can be lost or maybe even passed along to someone more faithful. Don't let that be your story. A meaningful career, a purpose-filled life, lies at the intersection of your God-given abilities and the needs of the world around you. When you serve others with your talents and give credit to God, you hit the sweet spot: a life that matters.

Focus Questions

1. What are some talents or abilities you've recognized in yourself? Have you been using them primarily for personal gain or for service to others and God?
2. When do you feel most "in the zone"? What activities bring you joy, energy, or a sense of purpose?
3. How has comparison, comfort, or fear shaped your work or life choices? Where might God be calling you to "choose the hard path" instead?
4. When you think about how you spend your time, do you feel like you're stewarding it well? What distractions might be keeping you from showing up fully and faithfully?

Do It Today

1. Write down five specific gifts, talents, or strengths God has given you. Don't overthink it—they can be big or small (public speaking, listening well, artistic skills, problem-solving, empathy, etc.)
2. Next to each gift, write one way you could use it this week to serve someone else, build something good, or honor God. Keep it simple and doable. ("Use my writing skill to send an encouraging email," "Use my hospitality to host a few friends," etc.)
3. Circle the one that resonates most—and do it this week. Don't wait for a perfect time. Don't worry about the applause. Do it for your audience of one.

Chapter 5

COMMUNITY MATTERS

You are the average of the five people you spend the most time with.

—ATTRIBUTED TO JIM ROHN

PEOPLE-SHAPED

Take a moment to read the quote above. Let's sit with that idea for a second. Sure, the truth is probably a bit more nuanced than this pithy little saying makes it seem, but the heart of it rings true, doesn't it?

I know some of you are thinking, *No way, not for me. I am who I am, and no one can change that.*

All right, boss man. If you say so.

But seriously, sure, I'll grant that there are people out there (and maybe you really are one of them) who aren't easily influenced by others. But as a general rule? Even if we tell ourselves that we're emotionally mature, spiritually grounded, independent thinkers who are above influence, the truth is the people closest to us create a little portable atmosphere that we carry around with us all day long. Whether you like it or not, the people you spend time with shape your decisions and beliefs, and yes, how you handle your money. And if you surround yourself with people who don't have the attitude, beliefs, and habits that you aspire to have? You'll find yourself becoming more and more like them: a version of yourself that you don't want to be.

Want to know where you're headed financially and spiritually? Look at your people. Want to know how generous you'll be, how frugal or extravagant, how content or discontent? Watch what your friends do with their time and money. The truth is, you'll almost never truly outgrow your circle. More often, your circle defines your ceiling.

Proverbs 27:17 says, *"As iron sharpens iron, so one person sharpens another."* That means relationships are never neutral. They either sharpen or dull, strengthen or weaken, build up or wear down.

In this chapter, we're going to talk about the people who shape us most: friends, spouses, mentors, and the family you grew up in.

FRIENDS: THE FORK IN THE ROAD

At some point in your life, you probably faced a pivotal choice—a fork in the road, if you will—about what friendships or friend group to really invest in. Maybe it happened in high school, maybe in college; maybe you were hyperaware it was happening, or maybe it just kind of crept up on you, and you barely realized you'd made a choice at all. Let's just see if this sounds familiar.

To your right was the path that would get you all intertwined with people who you deeply admired—people with serious, faithful attitudes, beliefs, and habits. Looking at this group, you knew joining their ranks would be a hard path, at least at first. Maybe you didn't know them very well yet; maybe they were more than a little intimidating, with all their earnest striving and put-togetherness. Hanging out with them, you knew, would push you to become a better version of yourself, and that would take serious work.

On the other hand (and you looked to your left), you could just follow the path that took you to those friends with the "bad" (more fun) attitudes, beliefs, and habits. The left path was going to be easy at first. It was the path of least resistance, maybe because these were people you were already familiar with, maybe just because it looked more comfortable and enjoyable.

But what if you could have seen into the future at that moment? What does your life look like now, five or ten years after the proverbial fork in the road?

Let's imagine you chose to go right at the fork. You started hanging out with people you admired. Notice I didn't say that you idolized them because they're flawed humans just like everyone else—but they do have the character qualities you find admirable. Maybe they do the following:

+ Don't stay out late partying.
+ Set their alarm clocks to get up early and have quiet time reading the Bible and praying.
+ Exercise in some form on a daily basis.
+ Have jobs and are disciplined with how they manage money.
+ Treat others, from restaurant staff to their girlfriends, with deep respect.

So fast-forward ten years: each of you is leading a meaningful life. You've earned college degrees and are working hard, and some of you have even become entrepreneurs because that's how you heard God calling you to use your gifts and talents for service and for his glory. This group doesn't have everything figured out, but when you look around, you notice *Wow, we are all* much *more content in life than most people our age.*

The relationships you and your friends have with your spouses are strong. In general, everyone in the group tries to stay fit and healthy. And you're all trying to be good stewards of the money God has entrusted you with by sensibly spending, prudently saving, avoiding debt, and generously giving. Even though your lives are busier than ever before, you stay connected through a weekly breakfast gathering. You all are still growing as individuals through mutual encouragement and accountability. The friendships persist, and so do the shared, beneficial habits and attitudes.

Now, back to the crossroads: let's say you chose to go left, taking the familiar, easy, and "fun" path. You and your friends stay out late several nights per week. On those nights, all of you have too much to drink and pay for it the next morning with hangovers that keep you in bed until noon, leading to missed classes. Ten years later, you're maybe finally graduating from college. With all the absences thanks to your "fun" nights out, it took you six years to earn your degree, which adds up to an extra $50,000 in student loan debt. You have to start paying that debt off ASAP, so you settle for a job you don't like. Since it's not remotely enjoyable or fulfilling, you spend your free time chasing happiness in the form of alcohol, binge-watching TV, stress-eating, and shopping. (This is starting to feel a bit like *If You Give a Mouse a Cookie*, isn't it?)

Are you still hanging out with that fun friend group? Well, you all graduated at different times, or not at all, so, nope, you lost contact with them. But did you make new friends? Eventually, maybe—but maybe not. For several years, you were so discouraged with life that you isolated yourself and defaulted to your past destructive lifestyle choices. So the friends are gone, and only the wasteful, harmful patterns remain.

Pause.

Is your life forever doomed if you choose the wrong "five people" to spend your time with? No, of course not. With God's grace and mercy, you can make a course correction. I'll spend more time exploring that idea at the end of this chapter, but I wanted to start with this little illustration to really communicate the importance of who you choose to surround yourself with.

The most important choice you'll ever make when it comes to relationships? Easy: it's all about who you marry. Your relationship with your spouse shapes your financial future.

ONENESS WITH YOUR SPOUSE

Now, here I need to take a minute to shout out my incredible wife. I cannot imagine how my life would have gone if I hadn't wound up with such a supportive, complementary partnership. Watching her thrive gives me joy, and I know she feels the same. That's what it's all about, isn't it? I can't overstate the importance of finding a good, faithful, and loving spouse: for the sake of life in general and (to return to the focus of the book) for your stewardship and financial health as well.

In Genesis 2:24, we read that a man shall *"leave his father and mother and hold fast to his wife, and they shall become one flesh."* That oneness includes intimacy, identity, and, yes, finances, too.

Toward the end of my last semester of college, my accounting professor (to this day, the wisest man I've ever met) announced that he wanted to send us seniors out into the world with sound money guidance that would serve us well for the rest of our lives. With that goal in mind, he told us, he had brought in a couple of guest speakers.

Our interest was piqued, and our expectations maybe soared a bit too high. Would it be someone like the prominent billionaires Warren Buffett and Bill Gates? Nope. Oh, what about brilliant and successful entrepreneurs like Elon Musk and Jeff Bezos? Wrong again. The professor welcomed a pair of familiar faces to the classroom: two of the college's staff members. They weren't even finance, business, accounting, or economics professors. One was an English professor, and the other was the university's conference services director.

So, just what made these two qualified to impart any resounding financial wisdom to such an astute group of young business-y minds? As we come to find out, they had been married for some ginormous number of years—happily married, I might add. Over my four years on campus, this couple always had a smile. They oozed contentment. It was palpable. What was their secret, and how did money play a role in their successful marriage? They took that whole "becoming one" thing seriously. One flesh, one heart, one mind—and one bank account. Mic drop.

This couple gave, saved, tithed, and dreamed as a unit, and that unity wasn't legalism or codependence—it was joyful. You could see the peace on their faces. They weren't competing or keeping score; they were in it as a team. They exemplified what God's design for marriage was supposed to look like, and because of their obedience, God blessed them. It's not easy to think of money in this unified way. We're inherently selfish creatures. From birth, we want what's ours to be only ours. As we embark on our marital journey, this deeply rooted instinct doesn't just miraculously go away. In fact, selfishness around money is one of the leading causes of divorce.

Let's contrast this lovely married pair with a fictional couple I just made up. We'll call them Jake and Claire.

Jake and Claire have decided to keep their finances separate: their bank accounts, their budgets, their savings goals. Claire grew up poor and wants security. Jake grew up wealthy and just wants to enjoy life. Without honesty and unity, every little thing has become a power struggle. There's a problem here that's about way more than money: it's about disconnection.

Let's say Jake and Claire have worked out a system that makes sense on paper. Each paycheck goes into their own personal account. They divide bills according to income—Claire, the higher earner, pays the mortgage, and Jake covers smaller utilities. They each pay their own credit cards, phone bills, and personal expenses.

This strategy seems reasonable on the surface, but watch how it blows up.

Claire, a traveling nurse, is on the road a lot, often spending north of a hundred nights a year away from home. One evening, tired from another week spent traveling, Claire arrives home to find a sink full of dirty dishes and Jake in the backyard cleaning his hunting rifle. Frustrated, she swings the back door open and gives Jake "the look."

"Hey, babe," cries an elated Jake, walking over to kiss her hello.

Claire dodges his hug, and he stops, his enthusiasm squelched in one fell swoop. The battle begins, and it quickly morphs into something that's not really about the dishes at all. Pretty soon, it's about unspoken expectations, insecurity, and financial imbalance.

Claire, feeling like she's having to carry the weight of both their home *and* their finances, makes a snarky remark about Jake's choice of work and lower income. Jake, feeling like his contributions are being belittled, lashes out about Claire's expensive shoe collection. He caught a glimpse of her credit card bill last week, and now he feels justified in thinking she has no right to point fingers when it comes to finances. Claire, in return, questions Jake's respect for her work. Suspicions flare, voices are raised, and hot diggity dog. We've officially gone off the rails. What should have been a peaceful evening has turned into a proxy war over finances—and identity.

Clearly, this is a hypothetical story, so I'm not going to fabricate a conclusion identifying Claire or Jake as the winner. I have no interest in ending a marriage—even a totally fictional one. But honestly, isn't it obvious here that there will never be a clear winner and that they will forever be at odds if they continue to keep their money separate? If only they could begin to think of their money as *theirs*, a common pool that they steward together with transparency and gratitude for one another's hard work, with no focus at all on who makes the most (because it's all shared), with open, honest communication, with common goals and a collaboratively-determined budget, man. That would make all the difference for poor Jake and Claire.

When couples keep finances separate, it often leads to secrecy, inequality, and misunderstanding. One partner might hide debt. The other might feel pressure to earn more or contribute more. The one earning more might dominate decisions, while the one managing the home might feel undervalued. One spouse might get into the destructive habit of complaining to a buddy about the other's spending habit, and suddenly, little things—like a dish left in the sink—become symbols of deeper division.

The most practical financial advice I can give married couples? Share your accounts and share your goals. Don't fight against each other—fight *for* each other. Do the dishes before they get crusty. Say thank you for the small things. It's rarely the big financial decisions that blow up a marriage. It's the slow leak of unspoken resentment that causes the most damage.

As the old saying goes, "Don't make a mountain out of a molehill." But if your finances are split down the middle, even the molehills can feel like Everest.

And by the way, here's a note on timing. The best moment to align financially is sometime *well* before the wedding. Financial baggage—debt, spending habits, credit scores—should not be surprises saved for the honeymoon. You know what can really ruin a beachside daiquiri? Discovering your new spouse has $40,000 in credit card debt they "forgot" to mention.

Full financial transparency builds trust. If you're engaged, I highly recommend finding a Christian premarital counselor who will walk you through these conversations. God designed marriage, so why not prepare for it using his wisdom?

And speaking of weddings, can we take a sec to talk about the cost?

According to *The Knot*, the average wedding today costs $33,000.[19] Add in the ring and honeymoon, and you're easily pushing $45,000. As a financial advisor, that number makes me throw up in my mouth a little. (Not full-on emoji vomit like the mind-boggling standard monthly car payment you see these days, but close.)

I get it—it's a once-in-a-lifetime event (hopefully). But come on. Is that kind of spending *really* necessary for you to cherish the day? Let me challenge you with this: what if you cut your wedding budget in half and invested the rest? Now, there's a way to start your marriage off with the right (financial) foot forward.

Marriage should be about how you spend your *life* together, not how *much* you spend on a *day*. Choosing the right spouse is the most important relational decision you'll ever make. This is the person you'll share a bed, a home, a future—and yes, a budget—with.

Get it right, and marriage becomes a foundation for peace, purpose, and generosity. Get it wrong, and it can become a source of constant friction.

Your spouse will shape your financial future more than any friend, colleague, or mentor ever will. That's why financial unity—real "one flesh" living—isn't just good advice. It's God's design.

MENTORS: WISDOM AND PERSPECTIVE

You and your spouse are a team, the primary unit at the heart of your financial decision-making and stewardship. But other voices influence the stewardship journey too. If you want to get your feet under you so you can move forward with confidence, find a mentor.

One of the fastest ways to grow—financially, spiritually, and emotionally—is to ask good questions of someone who's already walked the road. Not just anyone. Someone with purpose. Someone who has walked through both blessing and suffering and still trusts God.

Proverbs 15:22 says, *"Plans fail for lack of counsel, but with many advisers they succeed."*

You don't need a thousand opinions. You just need a few wise ones. Look for a mentor who

- ◆ manages money with integrity;
- ◆ walks closely with Jesus;
- ◆ lives the kind of life you actually respect; and
- ◆ tells the truth with gentleness.

Mentors help you see what you can't. Their wisdom can save you years of pain. And one day, you'll be able to do the same for someone else.

It's not just about finding someone ahead of you. Consider seeking the following:

- Someone ahead of you in the area you want to grow—whether that's financial stewardship, emotional maturity, or spiritual depth.
- Someone beside you, a peer walking through the same stage of life, to help you stay accountable and encouraged.
- Someone behind you who you can pour into and encourage.

If you didn't grow up with a parent, coach, or teacher who modeled wise money habits and played the role of mentor for you, it's not too late. Ask around. Look in your church. Talk to someone whose life bears good fruit. Don't be afraid to cold contact someone you admire and think you could learn from—the risk is worth it as long as you go at it with humility, respect, and confidence. You'll never know unless you ask, and you'd be surprised how many people would *love* to mentor someone younger. Honestly, they often get even more out of it than the mentee.

And remember—money is *so* personal. If someone's willing to talk to you about finances, odds are, they'll talk about all kinds of deeper things too, and that can be an invitation to grow in even deeper ways. Just be judicious with who you trust. Bad apples are out there, and you have to use your Spidey sense sometimes, but the good ones are very much all around as well.

Wise counsel is a gift. Don't go it alone.

FAMILY: THE INHERITANCE YOU CAN'T SEE

Most of us inherit our money mindset long before we ever earn a paycheck. Maybe your parents modeled generosity and trust in God. Maybe they modeled fear, control, or chaos. Either way, your family taught you something. Often, it's that inherited narrative that causes more financial struggle than the actual numbers.

If you grew up hearing, "We're just not good with money," or "Rich people are greedy," or "You owe us for helping you," then things like stewardship, planning, or even basic generosity might feel like betrayal. But here's the good news: *you* can be the fork in the road. You can honor your family while choosing a new story.

Maybe your parents never tithed, never saved, never planned for retirement. You can. Maybe your family always fought about money. You can choose peace. Don't let guilt drive your decisions. Don't let family pressure rob your future. You're allowed to set boundaries and still love well.

Proverbs 22:6 says, *"Train up a child in the way he should go; even when he is old, he will not depart from it."* But what if no one trained you? Then you get to be the one who starts the legacy.

Part of that legacy might include redefining what it looks like to help your family in a healthy way. You might feel compelled to support a relative who's going through a hard time. Be generous, but also be wise. I personally don't think "loaning" money to family or friends is helpful for either party. It introduces awkward power dynamics and often leads to resentment. (Thanksgiving's awkward enough. Let's keep the focus on faith, family, food, and football—not finances.)

Instead, when you're asked or feel led to help, pray about it. And if God puts it on your heart to give, then give freely, with no strings attached. But don't become an enabler. It shouldn't turn into a recurring pattern. If progress isn't being made, have an honest conversation. Offer support in other ways: encouragement, education, accountability.

You can love your family well without sacrificing your own financial health. You can choose both grace and wisdom. You can change the story—for yourself and for the generations to come.

COURSE CORRECTIONS

If you're reading this and realizing you've picked the wrong friends, started off on the wrong track entirely thanks to your parents, or are in a relationship with someone who you're out of alignment with, financially speaking—you're not doomed. You're just at a fork in the road, and God's inviting you to make a change.

You can reverse course, do an about-face, and start living your life according to his commands and not by your own selfish desires. Proverbs 16:9 says, *"The heart of a man plans his way, but the LORD establishes his steps."* Remember Jonah—you know, Jonah and the whale? God told him to go to Nineveh, and he ran in the other direction. But in Jonah 3:1, after the whole fish debacle, it says: *"Then the word of the LORD came to Jonah a second time."* That verse is so moving because it reminds us God doesn't just *allow* course corrections—he *calls* us to them.

God gave Jonah a second chance, a chance to course correct. He can do the same for you. If you got caught up with the wrong crowd and veered away from the right path, God, in his sovereignty, can put you back on the right path. He might even use your proximity to your former friends to change their lives too, like he did with Jonah's shipmates.

Start slow. Spend more time with people who challenge you to grow, and build some close friendships with people who you can talk openly and honestly with about money, holding one another accountable to manage finances wisely, calling one another out, and encouraging one another without any humble bragging. Join a group at church. Find a couple that has what you want in your marriage or finances and invite them to coffee. Pray before making big relational shifts. God cares about your community, and he designed us to grow through it.

Set healthy boundaries. Whether it's a friend who constantly mooches, a parent who guilts you about "what you owe," or a spouse with very different financial instincts, don't shy away from hard conversations. Set the table: "This is going to be personal and hard, but I want us to grow and hear each other out." Be honest, be kind, and know when to bring in wise counsel.

If you're married, picture a triangle: God at the top, you and your spouse at either end. As you each draw closer to God, you'll draw closer to each other. If tithing hasn't been part of your life, consider starting. It's not magic, but it's often the shift that resets our entire perspective on money. Try to get to the heart of the issue, determine if your differences are reconcilable, and don't give up: It's just money. You can always communicate more and compromise more for the good of the marriage.

If the issue is with friends, set boundaries. It might be time for some "necessary endings."[20] If it's family, love them—but recognize they aren't your spouse, and it's OK to agree to disagree. Scripture says to "leave your mother and father" and cleave to your spouse. That doesn't mean cutting ties, but it does mean redefining priorities.

And in all things—pray first. For wisdom. For peace. For courage. You don't need a massive overhaul overnight. But one small, intentional course correction can change the whole direction of your life.

CHOOSE YOUR PEOPLE, CHOOSE YOUR FUTURE

Now, after spending all this time talking about the importance of people, I've never once mentioned what a big old introvert I am.

People, honestly, drain me. I don't naturally gravitate toward relationship and community. But, oh boy: in the right dosage, over time, is it ever necessary. Service and friendship? Those bring joy. Consumerism and isolation? Definitely ain't it.

Just like me, as unwilling as I am, *you* were made for community—but not just any community. The right people will challenge you, sharpen you, and remind you of who you really are: God's child and a steward of God's great gifts. I pray this book will help you build friendships where honest conversations about money, marriage, and faith are normal.

Life's too short to walk alone or with the wrong crowd. Choose wisely. Choose prayerfully. In the end, your people shape your path.

Focus Questions

1. Think about the five people you spend the most time with. Who are they? How are they shaping your character, values, habits, and financial decisions?

2. If you're married (or planning to be), how aligned are you and your partner when it comes to money? Are there areas of financial disunity that need attention?

3. What kind of legacy did your family pass down around money, work, and generosity? What parts of that legacy do you want to carry forward—and what parts might need to stop with you?
4. Do you have a mentor (or mentors) speaking into your financial and spiritual life? If not, what's stopping you from seeking one?
5. What might God be asking you to course correct when it comes to your community? Is there a conversation, boundary, or new connection you need to initiate?

Do It Today

1. Write down the names of five people you spend the most time with right now.
2. Ask yourself three questions about each person:
   - Are they growing in character and wisdom?
   - Do they challenge me to become more generous, disciplined, and Christ-centered?
   - Do I leave conversations with them encouraged or depleted?
3. Pick one intentional action to strengthen your circle this week:
   - Invite a wise person to coffee and ask them to mentor you.
   - Set a healthy boundary with someone who drains your energy or encourages poor decisions.
   - Plan a quality moment (even just a call) with someone who makes you better.
   - Pray for wisdom about relationships that may need a course correction.

Part 3

THE BUILDING BLOCKS

Chapter 6

BUDGETING BY THE BOOK

Those who want to get rich fall into temptation and a trap and into many foolish and harmful desires that plunge people into ruin and destruction. For the love of money is a root of all kinds of evil. Some people, eager for money, have wandered from the faith and pierced themselves with many griefs.

—1 TIMOTHY 6:9–10

WHAT WE CAN LEARN FROM OUR TRASH (AND BANK ACCOUNTS)

You can tell a lot about someone by their trash. I don't just mean the literal banana peels and takeout containers—but what they bought, what they valued, what they wasted. It's kind of gross, but it's true. (Not that I spend a lot of time digging through people's dumpsters.) In the same way, your bank account might be telling a story *you're* not aware of.

Think about it. If someone had to describe you based solely on your spending, after taking a peek at your bank account's transaction log, what story would they tell? And be honest: would you be a little (or a lot) embarrassed to have them poking around in there?

Would they see someone who's generous and thoughtful? Impulsive and anxious? Would they see someone who's just surviving or someone building toward something better?

The goal here isn't to create shame but just to raise your awareness. Your spending habits are little fingerprints of your priorities—some intentional, some accidental. And here's the good news: once you see the story you've been telling with your money, if you don't like it? You can change the ending.

That's where budgeting comes in, not as a punishment or a prison but as a tool for clarity, freedom, and well-ordered priorities.

So don't look away. Log into your bank account. Scroll through your transactions. It might feel like reading a stranger's journal, but the stranger is you. Be curious. Be honest. Let yourself feel that bit of embarrassment, and then get hopeful. This is where the change starts.

WHAT'S IN A MINDSET? SCARCITY VERSUS ABUNDANCE

Before we dive into some practical habits and strategies for budgeting, let's talk about the difference between a biblical and a worldly view of money. I'm talking about mindsets, namely, the mindset of scarcity versus the mindset of abundance.

> **Scarcity mindset:** A way of thinking that focuses on what you don't have, and how little there is to go around in this world.

> **Abundance mindset:** A way of thinking that rests in trusting God's provision, and in the belief that his support and resources for all of us are infinite.

Whether you're on social media, watching the news, or talking to a friend about finances, you quickly pick up on the fact that we all tend to functionally believe that all the money in the world is kind of squashed together into one giant pie. It's this singular, finite thing, and it's only so big, and there's just not quite enough to go around. The natural human response? Anxiety. "There'll be none left over for me. I need to take as much as I can, as soon as I can." That's a scarcity mindset. If we approach finances thinking that way, is it any wonder we so easily fall into greed and workaholism or, conversely, into self-soothing apathy and poor spending habits?

But the thing is, we have a Savior who turned water into wine, who transformed a few bits of bread and fish into a feast that fed thousands. I firmly believe that we cannot even begin to comprehend the ways that God can and will provide for us if we step forward in faith. That means living out of an abundance mindset, putting others first with a generous heart, and trusting in his goodness to carry us through. *Even* when the practical realities of our time, economy, or personal situation seem to tell us to do just the opposite.

The pie isn't fixed. God's provision is bigger than we imagine. Before we begin to budget well, we need to unclench our hearts a little bit and commit to living out of a place of generous, trusting abundance.

AVOIDING LIFESTYLE CREEP: LIVE WITHIN YOUR MEANS

Of course, I'm not saying you should approach your money with reckless swagger and unwise wastefulness. Quite the contrary. When we deal with money, we should certainly prioritize generosity and trust in God to provide for our needs, *as long as we also steward what we've been given well.*

So, to do that? We start from a place of contentment rather than comparison. Easier said than done, I know. But think about the power of combining an abundance mindset—one that trusts there is enough to go around, that allows you to live generously with a focus on serving others rather than worrying if you'll get your piece of the pie—with an attitude of true contentment. I'm talking about an attitude that allows you to look at your life and smile without much thought for how it measures up against your friend's life, that influencer's life, that celebrity's life—even your parents' lives. (Because so often, we look at where our parents *ended up* and expect to *start there*—a crazy expectation.)

That combination of abundance mindset and contentment is going to be what helps you to live successfully within your means, avoiding the lifestyle creep that is so prevalent for members of the youngest generations today: that tendency to make bigger purchases than make sense, living in bigger houses and driving better cars than you can really afford, all for the sake of appearances, or simply because you've gotten accustomed to the luxury. You won't be spurred on by anxiety over not getting your piece of the pie, and you won't be driven mad by comparison and discontent with what you *do* have. You'll find you have more than enough and peace of mind as well.

But when you *don't* cultivate that mindset? It's so easy to spend more than you have on a regular basis without really thinking about it.

During my early twenties, I was still trying to work on my tact, especially with my wife. One thing that used to always drive me crazy—that I just could *not* seem to keep my mouth shut about—was when she would have a day off work, and she'd decide to spend it shopping.

Being a sports fan, I routinely find myself drawing parallels between sports and real life, and this situation was no exception. When my wife would choose to go shopping on her day off, it always made me think of a rare but impactful football play called a "pick six." A pick six is when an opposing player intercepts a pass and runs it back the other way for a touchdown. The way I pictured it, income was *our* endzone. When you head to work, off to make some money, that's you driving down the field toward a touchdown. But then: a day off hits. Instead of making that money (scoring that touchdown), you lose possession of the ball, and you don't stop there. You take it further and even *spend* money, letting the ball slip back toward the *other* endzone and allowing the opposing team to score a touchdown. What could be worse than not just not making money but actively losing it at the same time?

I've learned not to nitpick this particular habit of my wise and otherwise frugal wife, if only because my passive-aggressive mutterings about the pick six always earned me the evil eye. But to continue looking at someone besides myself for examples of counterproductive money habits (and what better target than the woman I love best in the world?): have you heard of *girl math*?

Let's say my wife is graciously given, out of the kindness of their capitalist hearts, ten dollars off her next purchase of fifty dollars or more from a clothing retailer. Here's girl math in action: "I *need* to use this ten dollars by the end of the weekend before it expires and I *lose* it." So my wife proceeds to browse the retailer's website, intent on finding a way to spend that ten dollars. She finally finds something she kind of likes, but it's only forty-nine dollars (how coincidental), and she has to throw in a five-dollar pair of socks (that will get lost in her sock drawer within two weeks) to rise above the $50 threshold. With tax and all, she's now spent fifty dollars—*after* the ten-dollar "gift" from the retailer.

Before she was "given" the ten dollars, was she searching that retailer's website in hopes of loading the cart with fifty dollars' worth of clothes? Absolutely not. The retailer provided the bait on the hook, my wife took the bait, and then she proceeded to use girl math to justify the purchase. This is just one more example of the little ways we trick ourselves into acting out of a place of scarcity and discontentment—one of the little moments that can add up to lifestyle creep and a long-lasting cycle of spending more than you have.

By the way, guys, you're not off the hook. We obviously have ways of justifying our overspending, too. If you tend to measure your own worth by what you achieve, chances are you're eager to show *others* what you've achieved, as well. You go fishing and catch a big fish? You take a picture to show it off. Kill a deer? Mount it prominently on the wall for your guests to see. Win a race? Here's a medal. You get the point: we like to show off to make sure people know we're good or successful at something.

That impulse seeps into our buying choices. The clearest examples are houses and cars. Now, my generation grew up with shows like *MTV Cribs*. This show featured celebrities providing viewers with a tour of their lavish homes and lifestyles. The main takeaway: if you're successful, you drive a fancy car and live in a big house. That's a real temptation and one that can really mess up your finances for a long time if you give into it and make a *huge* purchase you can't really afford.

If you find yourself in either of the two camps, using girl math or letting pride affect your buying choices, remember the issue is larger than just this single, weak moment. It's about where your heart is and where your head is.

Cultivate abundance and cultivate contentment. Live within your means, and you'll be off to a wonderful start.

BEATING THE (MARKETING) VOICES

My six-year-old recently made me laugh out loud. He found his ears inundated with an ad for something while we were driving one day, and after listening intently for a moment, he exclaimed, "Aww, they're just trying to get you to *buy* something!"

Being aware of the tricks and gimmicks of marketing is half the battle.

I really had my eyes opened when I saw a breakdown of the kinds of cognitive biases[21] marketers exploit to get us clicking Buy Now:

- **Anchoring bias:** when you rely on the *first* piece of information you receive (like when the sight of the "original" price makes the discount seem far more reasonable).
- **Recency effect:** when you give more weight to the latest information you received (your sink springs a leak, and you immediately think of the ad for a plumber you just heard on the radio that morning).
- **Authority bias:** when you trust the opinions of those you perceive as authorities (so a product endorsed by a real doctor, politician, or celebrity gets your attention every time).
- **Bandwagon effect:** when you do what everyone else is doing (so you're a sucker for the brands pumping out the cheap but oh-so-cool styles all your friends are wearing).

Cognitive bias: A thought pattern that causes us to see reality incorrectly; basically, when we let our own brains fool us.

From a capitalistic standpoint, I get it. It is what it is: businesses exist to make a profit, and to do that they've got to try and get you with their sneaky little marketing emails and ads, with their ten-dollars-off coupons like the one my wife used in the story above, and so on. But my goodness, in the context of social media and our phones, especially, marketing has gotten downright predatory.

If you have a text conversation with someone and mention needing new pickleball shoes, your screen suddenly prompts you with an Apple Pay icon to the listing you mentioned, and you can bet there'll be new ads waiting for you the next time you open a social media app. We get texts on a daily basis informing us of incredible sales (but are they really sales if the price has pretty much always been fifty-nine dollars, and that "Marked down 20 percent!" announcement is just for looks?). We can purchase pretty much anything with just one click, while we're sitting in the drive-through line or even super quickly at a red light. And don't even get me started on the prompts like "People Also Bought" or "Need Anything Else Before You Check Out?" that pop up so frequently during online shopping. It's become insidious, hasn't it?

But you can stave off the onslaught. Really, you can. Start by simply becoming aware of *when you're being tricked and coerced.* Ads are the enemy—don't let them beat you. If there's a struggle going on, and someone's trying to exploit you, it's on you to take the reins and stop them. And then, after you've really developed your awareness of the different marketing tricks and tactics, shift your focus to cultivating small habits.

LITTLE HABITS

The good habits we nurture around spending and budgeting have a whole lot to do with the difference between short-term and long-term thinking.

Our current youngest generations, more than any others before them, have been programmed to expect instant gratification. Think same-day delivery, subscription services, instant access to any movie you can think of through ad-free streaming, and the easy discovery of any book you like via e-readers. Our attention spans have been clipped down to almost nothing thanks to social media reels, and we can communicate, buy and sell, calculate, do homework, and be guided from point A to point B (without actually having to study and plan the route out on the map) using our handheld smartphones. The world is at our fingertips. No wonder older people describe today's young people as the "microwave" generation.

It makes me think of poor old Esau, who sold his birthright for a bowl of soup.[22] In the moment he made that decision, I'm sure he didn't think he was in danger of making a foolish, impulsive choice. He was *hungry—so* hungry, he cried to his brother, that he would surely die.

When our emotions get mixed up or intensified, and our desires take on the appearance of urgent needs—"I *need* some pizza! I *need* the newest smartphone! I *need* a luxury vacation!"—it becomes hard to think about anything past that short-term impulse. Ring a bell?

So, what habits can we build to help us fight that short-term impulsivity and lack of wisdom around spending?

+ **A weekly spending check-in.** Sometimes, we just aren't paying attention. If you'd realized that you'd already spent eighty dollars on takeout, a hundred dollars on Amazon, and thirty dollars on convenience store snacks this week, well, you definitely wouldn't have clicked Buy Now on those jeans you really didn't need. Set up a day every week when you have to go through your purchases. Even if you don't fully tally them all up, a quick look can provide a wake-up call when it's most needed.

- **The twenty-four-hour spending rule.** You have constant access to a million websites selling this, that, and the other thing. See something you want? Make a commitment to wait a full day—twenty-four hours—before making the purchase. Creating guardrails can help you stay disciplined and in control of your decisions rather than allowing your emotions and desires to take over. Of course, this is easier said than done—but once the habit is ingrained, it's a powerful one.
- **Take your cards off your phone.** Got Apple Pay, Google Pay, whatever? Have your card linked to your Uber Eats account, your shipping address all set up to autofill? Take it all off. Keep your credit card and debit card in your wallet only, and make it a pain to have to go and grab it and enter all your personal information any time you decide to buy something. Maybe, in that moment of pause, you'll realize you don't really need it.
- **Block ads.** If you spend a second looking at a product on your phone, or if you're just existing, things you like and want (and, you tell yourself, things you *need*) are going to be advertised anytime you use your phone. There are multiple ways to combat this constant temptation: disabling third-party cookies, using an ad blocker, selecting "Ask App Not to Track" when prompted, or, heck, here's a crazy idea: get off social media and the sites that are the main culprits of this nonstop marketing stream.
- **Use cash and avoid recurring payments.** Nothing makes money real like using real money.

CREATING A BUDGET THAT WORKS: 10/10/80

You're set up with the mindsets and habits you need: now, how do you actually create a budget?

There are websites and books packed with advice on this topic, but if you want my two cents? The simple 10/10/80 method is the way to go:

- **Give** 10 percent of your income (No matter how much you make. Seriously. More on that later).

- **Save** 10 percent of your income.
- **Spend** the remaining 80 percent of your income on your daily expenses.

Now, this is a starting point. Over time, as you get better and better at avoiding lifestyle creep, you can increase your giving and saving while decreasing the amount you spend.

Here's my final tip: you need an organized way to track where your money is going. Don't skip this step and try to wing it—accurate measuring is vital. There are plenty of apps out there that make this task easy, including one I designed specifically for faithful young adults like you: the Purpose Planner. Give it a Google, scan the QR code below, or check the back pages of this book for more info.

While the mindsets, habits, and budgeting framework shared in this chapter can all act as helpful guidelines, remember that your money problems can never fully be solved with math equations. Money is personal. Money is emotional. But most importantly, money is spiritual. God knows that our relationship with money, if left unchecked, can lead to it becoming our idol. The passage I used to open this chapter bears repeating:

> *Those who want to get rich fall into temptation and a trap and into many foolish and harmful desires that plunge people into ruin and destruction. For the love of money is a root of all kinds of evil. Some people, eager for money, have wandered from the faith and pierced themselves with many griefs.* (1 Timothy 6:9–10)

Our relationship with money is a heart issue. Finding a healthy balance between wise financial stewardship and radical generosity is a lifelong journey, and early on, our lack of experience can lead to a super common pitfall: deep, deep debt. Let's examine biblical strategies and postures for dealing with *that* particular problem in more detail next.

Focus Questions

1. If someone judged your values by your spending over the last thirty days, what story would they tell? What do you *wish* that story said?
2. What "justifications" (a.k.a. girl math, guy pride, emotional buying, etc.) do you tend to use to talk yourself into purchases?
3. What marketing tricks tend to work on you? (Sales? Limited-time offers? Influencer recs? Autofill checkouts?) How can you resist them?
4. Do you have any weekly or monthly financial habits in place right now? Which of the suggested small habits or systems (weekly check-in, twenty-four-hour rule, 10/10/80 rule, etc.) feels most realistic for you to start?

Do It Today

1. Pull up your bank app and look at your last seven days of transactions.
2. Categorize each purchase as *need, want,* or *give.*
3. Reflect on the balance you observe. Are you happy with it? What needs to shift?
4. Choose one habit to implement this week:
   □ Set a calendar reminder for a weekly spending check-in.
   □ Use the twenty-four-hour rule for *any* non-essential purchase.
   □ Remove your card info from your phone and browsers.
   □ Block ads or reduce your screen time by thirty minutes/day.

Chapter 7

AVOIDING DEBT

Let no debt remain outstanding, except the
continuing debt to love one another.

—ROMANS 13:8

THE DEBT TRAP

Debt is so much more than a simple math problem. It's a serious emotional, spiritual, and financial weight. It hovers over your day-to-day decisions, colors your relationships, and limits your freedom. Scripture is clear on this: *"The borrower is slave to the lender"* (Proverbs 22:7). God doesn't warn us about debt to steal our fun, but because he desires financial freedom and peace for us. Being debt-free allows you to freely, cheerfully give with the generosity we are called to embrace. Margin in your finances—what you make outweighing what you spend, what you own outweighing what you owe—is what ultimately gives you margin in every area of life. It's what creates space to breathe, to invest in relationships and hobbies and yourself, and so much more. Instead of being stressed out of your mind and busy churning out that overtime to catch up on the bills, you can spend more time with your family and friends, focusing on your walk with God, volunteering for causes close to your heart, and all that good stuff.

But let's be honest: debt is so incredibly common these days that it's kind of just accepted as the norm at this point. Even though its burden is so powerful, society, corporations, and hustle-culture gurus are actively trying to convince you that it's fine and good. "It's a powerful wealth-building tool," they tell you. They use the term "leverage" and categorize some debt as bad—depreciating assets, the things you own that lose value with age, like your car—and some as good, like real estate or a growing business. That can be convincing when you're only looking at the numbers, but that view doesn't take the negatives of risk and financial stress into account. When the economy goes south? *All* debt is bad, in the end, and the game of risk and reward is rarely truly worth playing. As Warren Buffet famously said, "Only when the tide goes out do you discover who's been swimming naked."[23] Want to sleep well at night, without even a shadow of doubt over whether the debt you have will turn out to be the "good" or "bad" kind? Aim to have none at all—or very little, at most. Doing so will provide you with a level of peace that *more* than offsets any potential gains received from the leveraged strategies being touted so enthusiastically nowadays.

But, yep, in society at large, debt has been treated as a normal, acceptable thing for a long time, and the pandemic shook everything up for the average taxpayer even more. COVID stimulus checks, lifestyle upgrades, inflation? It all just snowballed. At the time of this writing, the cost of living is up. Interest rates are high. Many of us, maybe you included, have gotten used to a certain lifestyle, even if it meant borrowing to maintain it—and now you're trapped.

But it doesn't have to stay that way.

IS DEBT INEVITABLE?

I'll say it again: no. It's not. Even though it's been normalized, even though I am positive you, as you read this, have at least some level of debt—maybe you have a *lot*, an amount that is making you full-on panic—I want you to take this to heart. You are *not* doomed. You're *not* stuck. You can get out of debt. You can start now.

Shame is a terrible motivator—it paralyzes us. Debt is a beast, sure, but like the old saying goes: "How do you eat an elephant? One bite at a time." Take a deep breath. Let the stress motivate you to move and not to freeze, spiral, or give up.

We're going to dive deep into a few kinds of debt in a moment, but the basic principle for all of them is similar: avoid them. And if you're in the thick of debt of any sort, do all you can to get out of it ASAP. You have your whole life ahead of you, and you can do this. Take steps knowing you can't change things dramatically and immediately, but you will get through it. Take multiple jobs if you have to. If you don't start now, you'll find yourself in a deeper hole later.

Whether you're in $1,000 of credit card debt or six figures of student loans, the principle is the same: start today. Momentum is everything.

CREDIT CARDS

Ahh, credit cards: such a special and uniquely evil invention of the modern world.

I'm not being totally serious there. In truth, I sit somewhere squarely in between those savvy finance bloggers who provide tips on absolutely milking credit card points to the moon and good old David Ramsey with his hot "credit card execs have a direct line to the devil" take on the subject.

I don't actually think credit cards are inherently evil at all. Used responsibly, they can have their place in a wise and balanced financial life. But they are *incredibly* dangerous, especially in immature or unaware hands. (And credit card companies know this and exploit their users' weaknesses as hard as they can.)

In fact, credit cards are a whole lot like alcohol: not inherently bad, maybe, but akin to playing with fire. If you're not careful, what starts with a harmless tap here and there becomes a habit that ruins your budget and peace of mind. And, just like with alcohol, most people are introduced to credit cards when they're young and still developing healthy habits—hello, free t-shirt table on your college campus.

Credit cards are ultraconvenient. They're *too* convenient. You access them with one easy click at checkout, and they're linked to Apple Pay, Uber Eats, and every online store. When you get the added incentive of points and perks baked in, muddying the water between what you actually should be spending, your habits can balloon like crazy.

Even if you're someone who pays off your balance each month, studies show people still spend more when using credit.[24] So here's the rule: if you're going to use credit cards, treat them like your checking account. Track every single purchase. Like we discussed in the budgeting chapter, plan to do a weekly spending pie chart review (most banks and budgeting apps—like the Purpose Planner—will categorize things for you). And if you don't trust yourself, don't use credit cards at all. Crazy idea, I know, but you really can do it.

So here's the bottom line: use credit cards at your own risk. And never carry a balance—credit card interest rates are often in the 20 percent range. Compound interest is your friend when you're investing, but it's your worst enemy when it's working against you. Take a look at the included chart, and you'll see exactly how bad it can get.

Credit Card Interest Compounding
($5,000 at 20% APR, No Payments, 5 Years)

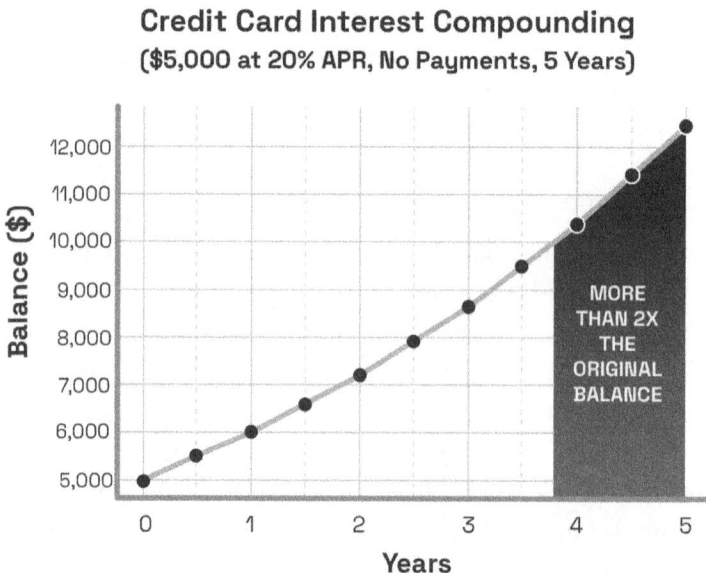

Shows how a $5000 balance grows over 5 years
if unpaid at 20% APR.

> **Compound interest:** Interest calculated **not only** on the initial, principal amount (e.g., the $100 you put on your credit card for those shoes you didn't need), but also on the additional, accumulated interest from previous periods (e.g., $100 + 25 percent of 100 = $125 last month—and this month, $125 + 25 percent of 125 = $156.25).

AUTO LOANS

OK, I'm adamant about this one, and it may have you categorizing me alongside Dave Ramsey as a tad old-fashioned: I believe you should *never* take on debt for a car. Cars are not investments—they're everyday tools that lose value the second you drive off the lot. In fact, most new cars depreciate 20–30 percent in the first year alone. Even with cash in hand, I still wouldn't buy new.

I do get that cars can be emotional. Ads make them look like status symbols. Commercials show us powerful trucks climbing mountains or luxury sedans with big red bows on Christmas morning. But at the end of the day, it's just a vehicle. It's not impressing anyone. You don't need a $60,000 SUV to drive your kids to soccer.

Most people think in terms of monthly payments: "Can I afford $450/month for this car?" But dealers *know* this and exploit it, and they will stretch your loan over six or seven years just to keep your monthly payment low, convincing you you've found a good deal. But in doing so, you massively overpay for the car when you consider all that interest that builds up over time.

Car Depreciation Over 10 Years

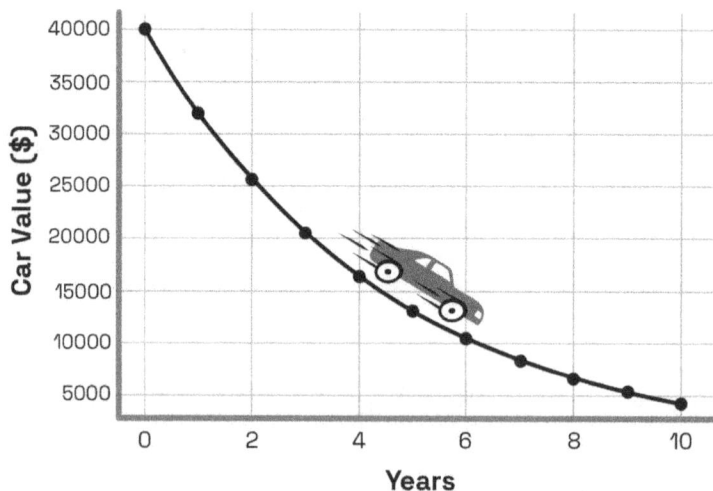

Depicts how a typical new car loses value—
about 20% per year on average

Instead of taking on the interest that comes along with a monthly payment, *start saving now.* Set aside money each month in a car fund. When you have enough, buy used—and buy with cash.

And don't forget the hidden costs: insurance, maintenance, repairs. The fancier the car, the fancier the bill. Humble wheels, no payment, and less stress: that's the goal.

STUDENT LOANS

A college education is important, but so are plain old common sense and wisdom. This section is for you high school-aged readers, and I want to start with a statement you may find hard to believe: you can earn a college degree with little to no student debt.

Since 1980, the cost of college has risen nearly 1,200 percent, whereas general inflation has risen by about 300–400 percent in the same period.[25] Why's there such a huge discrepancy? Increased demand, reduced public funding, administrative bloat, and ironically, easy access to federal loans that colleges know students will use—so they adjust their rates accordingly.

So where does that leave us? We're at an important point: it's become clear that, in general, college has become too expensive. Parents and students alike have become more selective in how they make higher education decisions, and the good news is we have lots of options.

Student debt is debt—which means it is worth avoiding. While everyone may follow a different path when it comes to higher education, here are my tips for navigating the process with your sights set on gaining a valuable education, student loan-free.

- Consider starting with community college or a tech school for your general education courses. It might be hard to resist the siren song of your dream college, but you can always transfer there once you've taken advantage of a more affordable option for those basic credits.

- Prioritize going to a school with in-state tuition. I know. You want to get out of your humdrum hometown and see the rest of the country, but seriously, that can wait. The difference between in-state and out-of-state tuition can be massive.

- Earn AP or dual-enrollment credits, or both, while you're still in high school.

- Apply for FAFSA as early as you can.

- Proactively hunt out scholarship opportunities. You never know what's out there till you do the research.

- Try to find an on-campus job or work-study to support your tuition.

- If you can, be a commuter: live at home. Dorm life may sound fun, but a place to stay that's free of charge *and* free of distractions will be priceless if you have that option. (But please, even if you decide to live at home, learn how to do your own laundry. You can and should learn those adulting skills, even if you don't move out.)

- If you don't have the option to live at home, find a quality friend to share expenses with as a roommate.

- Take summer classes.

- Be intentional and judicious about your major, and prioritize the classes you need to take in order to graduate as soon as possible.
- Not sure you're ready to make that thoughtful, purposeful choice yet? Take a gap year to work and explore your options.

Some argue college isn't worth it anymore. And sure, it's not the right path for everyone. But statistically, higher education still correlates with higher net worth. It's not about chasing wealth—it's about building margin and opportunity. Choose the right path for you—but choose it with your eyes wide open.

MORTGAGES

Homeownership is definitely a worthy goal. But don't confuse that normal, commonsense dream with the Instagram version of it.

Most young adults today want a home like the one they grew up in—forgetting that it took their parents twenty years to get there. The average house in the 1980s was 1,740 square feet. Today, it's over 2,500 square feet[26]—even though household sizes are actually getting smaller, with fewer and fewer people living in an average house even though the "average house" has ballooned in size.

Our expectations have ballooned, and our budgets are groaning under the weight of them.

Here are the basics:

- If you can, get a fifteen-year fixed mortgage, not a thirty-year. It'll save you tens of thousands in interest and free you up faster.
- Put 20 percent down if possible to avoid having to pay for PMI (private mortgage insurance).
- Don't buy too much house. You'll be encouraged to borrow the amount that the bank says you can afford: they'll give you more than what you'll want to be responsible for paying back on a monthly basis. They approve based on gross income, but you live on net income.

- Keep your monthly mortgage at or below 25 percent of your take-home pay. You need margin more than anything, and if that means living in a smaller, older house than you think is ideal? Do it.

> **Private mortgage insurance (PMI):** A type of insurance borrowers must pay to protect lenders on conventional mortgages when the down payment is less than 20 percent of the home's value. If you put down a smaller down payment, this additional cost can add a few hundred dollars a month to your living expenses.

And don't forget to calculate what you can afford with the expectation that you'll be hit with additional or hidden costs: property taxes, utilities, HOA fees, maintenance, and the costs of that social pressure to keep up with the Joneses. A too-big house often brings big expectations—and big headaches.

As I've already shared, I once bought a beautiful home with far more space than we needed, and I found I quite literally couldn't live with the guilt I felt over the wastefulness. When we sold it and downsized, I had no regrets.

A quick note here: I really hammered down on the evils of debt above, and now I'm encouraging you to take out a mortgage, the biggest debt of all? Here's the thing. You can save up enough for a car, but most people just aren't going to manage to save up a quarter of a million dollars in their twenties. And though renting for a while makes total sense, especially if you're single, buying a house makes *more* sense—*if* you do it wisely, as described above—when you're starting a family and getting into the swing of things career-wise. Just my two cents.

GETTING UNSTUCK

But let's say all this advice is coming a tad too late for you. You've already racked up some of the types of debt described above, and you're feeling overwhelmed and unsure how to get out from under it so you can reclaim some margin.

Let me just reiterate: there's hope. With some wisdom, diligence, strategy, and prayer, you can find your way out.

There are two commonly recommended strategies for tackling debt:

- **The debt avalanche**: Focus on the highest-interest debt first.
- **The debt snowball**: Focus on the smallest balance first.

I recommend the snowball method. Why? Because money is *emotional.* Targeting small debts that you can pay off relatively quickly gives you that shot of motivation and momentum you need to continue. Wins matter, and once you get a taste of progress, you're more likely to keep going.

The math nerds out there will tell you that the avalanche method ultimately saves you more in interest—and they're right. But this isn't just about straightforward equations. It's about freedom and what's going to actually help you to change your life. In that sense, I'd argue that momentum beats math.

Your home isn't a hedge fund. Your family isn't a startup. Take the slow, steady route. Build margin. Build peace.

When you're debt-free, you'll sleep better. You'll be more generous. You'll have a time margin, not just a financial margin. That's the kind of wealth worth pursuing.

Focus Questions

1. What kinds of debt (if any) are you currently carrying? How does that debt make you feel—financially, emotionally, spiritually?
2. Have you bought into the idea of "good debt" versus "bad debt"? How has that belief influenced your financial decisions?

3. Which type of debt (credit cards, auto, student loans, mortgage) feels most overwhelming or tempting to you? Why?
4. Which repayment strategy makes the most sense for you: avalanche (highest interest first) or snowball (smallest balance first)? Why?

Do It Today

1. Catalog your debts (yes, all of them), including the balance, interest rate, and minimum monthly payment.
2. Choose your strategy: snowball (targeting the smallest debts first) or avalanche (targeting highest interest first), and order the debts accordingly.
3. Make one move today:
   □ Set up an automatic extra payment (as little as twenty-five dollars or as much as you can manage) on your first target.
   □ Cancel one subscription (or commit to changing one frequent spending habit, like ducking into the gas station store for a Mountain Dew, hot dog, and box of Ho-Hos for lunch every day) and reroute that money toward the first target.
   □ Call your credit card company to see if you're eligible for a lower interest rate.
   □ Cancel or cut up a credit card entirely.

Chapter 8

GENEROUS GIVING

Bring your full tithe to the Temple treasury so there will be ample provisions in my Temple. Test me in this and see if I don't open up heaven itself to you and pour out blessings beyond your wildest dreams. For my part, I will defend you against marauders, protect your wheat fields and vegetable gardens against plunderers.

—MALACHI 3:10-11 (THE MESSAGE)

GREED, GREED, GREED

We live in a greedy world.

Early in my career, I was at a meeting with a bunch of industry peers. We were all sharing our stories of how we got into the business. A man across the room from me stood up and boldly declared his reason for getting out of bed every day: "I really, really like money."

He went on to list some of his recent purchases, including a wildly expensive new piano. He was not even a little bit embarrassed to declare that he worked hard every day with the single goal of earning as much money as he could so he could buy anything and everything he wanted, stuffing himself with pleasure and comfort until he'd had his fill.

Which, of course, he never would. I felt dirty listening to him, and the thing is that he's not alone. We all feel that pull toward greed, at least from time to time.

We've already talked about the huge difference you'll see between a life lived with a scarcity mindset and one lived with an abundance mindset. When you get it in your head that there's only so much pie to go around, grabbing as much as you can before everyone else gets to it becomes a serious temptation. We want to hoard, to make sure we have "enough," to make sure we have more than somebody else so we don't feel small, to tell ourselves we're worth something because of what we have.

It's all nonsense. It's worse than nonsense: it's a poison, and it can kill the spark of good, loving generosity God placed in all our hearts.

- ◆ "I don't have enough money to feel comfortable yet—I can't afford to give any away."
- ◆ "I'm working hard for what I want—I don't have time for anyone else."
- ◆ "I want to be a winner—why would I give someone else a hand in this race and fall behind for their sake?"

THE ANTIDOTE

If you spend much time around kids, you know how nice it is to see a couple little friends make the happy choice to share their favorite toys or snacks. It makes me so proud as a parent when I catch my children, uncoerced, being generous with one another—because it's not an easy thing to do. (Especially when Skittles or Magna-Tiles are involved.) It's even harder to be generous as a child when there's not a little friend standing in front of you asking you to share. My kids have "give," "save," and "spend" jars, and I remember the warm feeling of pride that swelled up in me one day when I saw my young daughter move money out of her "spend" jar (sacrificing a new book or stuffed animal) because she realized her "give" jar was empty, and she wanted to be able to tithe at church the next day.

If it gives us such a kick to see our own little ones loving one another through generosity and unselfishness, just think how happy it makes our heavenly Father to see us do the same.

Cheerful giving is the antidote to greed. Notice I don't just say "giving." I mean *cheerful* giving. Not grudging giving or giving done out of obligation but giving that pours out of a place of gratitude and abundance and love of our neighbors and our God. The happiest people I've ever known have always also been the most generous. It is truly more blessed to give than to receive.

How do you partake of that blessing? You just do it. Stop depending on money, and surrender your life to God through giving.

THE TITHE: WHAT DOES GOD ASK OF US?

So, how much should *you* give?

We've covered the 10/10/80 rule, and if you grew up in the church you were probably already familiar with that number—10 percent—as a giving guideline. That number isn't just something a pastor pulled out of thin air one day.

Leviticus 27:30 tells us this: *"A tenth of the produce of the land, whether grain or fruit, is the LORD's, and is holy."* The word "tithe" literally means "tenth." And the word "holy" means "set apart." That tenth is for nothing else but God and his work. Pretty straightforward, then: you should give 10 percent of whatever you make as a starting point and give even more as you're able.

So, as a kid making ten dollars in chore earnings each week, you placed a single dollar bill in the offering plate every Sunday; today, as an adult earning $80,000, it should look something like $150 a week. Simple, right?

But hang on, that's a lot of money. Should you be calculating that 10 percent before or after your salary's been taxed? Also, you're a good steward, so you thought ahead and signed up for your company's 401K plan as well, and a health savings account, life insurance, dental insurance, and all the other kinds of insurance we seem to need these days. A nice chunk of your paycheck is being deducted long before any money ever reaches you. Is God getting 10 percent of your gross pay or the net that actually makes it to your bank account? And even after that, shouldn't you be making sure your essential bills are paid first? God will understand that you've got to prioritize those student loans over tithing, right?

Gross pay: The total amount you earn before any deductions.

Net pay: The amount that actually reaches your pocket after taxes, retirement contributions, health insurance payments, and so on have been deducted from your paycheck.

First Paycheck Breakdown

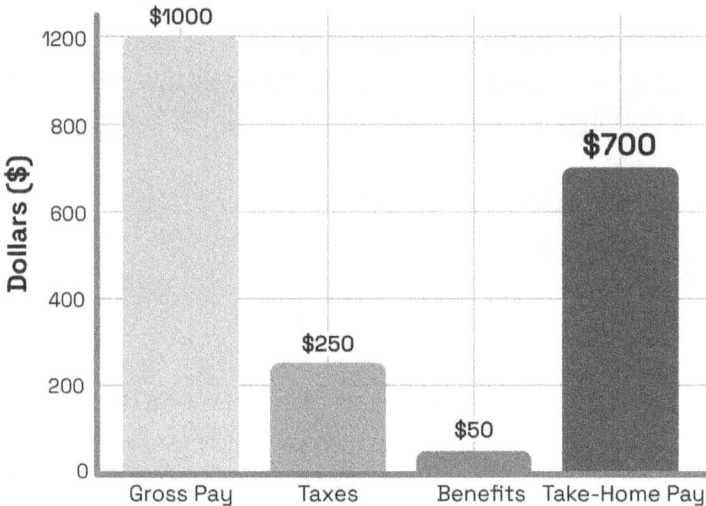

Illustrates how taxes and benefits reduce gross income to take-home pay

Oh, the games we play with God. We rationalize our thoughts and actions to make ourselves feel better, but deep down, we know what is right; we know what obedience looks like.

I'm a firm believer that 10 percent means 10 percent of *everything*, no matter what. It's all God's anyway, right? So we're called to give just a little slice of it back to him. Proverbs 3:9 says, *"Honor the LORD with your wealth, with the first fruits of all your crops." First* fruits. Not the last batch, once you've made sure you have enough to cover your butt. We honor God when we trust *him* with that grand task. That means letting go of at least 10 percent of *everything* we make, no matter how much that is, no matter how much disappears before it reaches us, no matter what.

When we tithe from our gross pay, even if things are tight, as an act of faith and obedience, the transactional exercise of tithing becomes a transformational spiritual practice. God doesn't want (or need) our money. He wants our hearts, and we give them to him when we relinquish control and step forward in faith.

DON'T LET FEAR STOP YOU

We church-goers today give a smaller percentage of our incomes (less than 3 percent) than our ancestors did during the Great Depression of the early 1930s.[27] Can you believe that? We're less generous than the people experiencing the Dust Bowl and breadlines were, even in the midst of their suffering. What on earth is keeping us so tight with our money?

Aside from the culture-wide greed we've already discussed, I believe the source of our hesitancy lies in fear. Did you know today's generation of young adults, Gen Z, has been nicknamed the Anxious Generation? According to a recent Barna study, about two in five Gen Zers report *always* feeling uncertain about the future, anxious about important decisions, and afraid to fail.[28] Not just sometimes: *always*. Does that resonate with you?

I think there are several reasons for this high anxiety level, this fear of instability that negatively impacts today's young adults' willingness to risk financial security through bold giving. The first is the intensified and expanded power of social pressure. Big thanks to the internet for that one, making the possibility of catastrophic financial failure all the more terrifying by convincing us to expose our daily lives to strangers. You've grown up in an age where peers, fueled by what I call "keyboard courage," feel free to bash each other through social media, saying things they'd never say to someone in person. Of *course*, the fear of failure has intensified: it's no longer just "What do the people I know think of me?" but "What does the entire population of the internet world think of me?"

On top of that, many members of this generation rarely experienced truly risky situations during their childhood and teenage years. Is that true for you? Did your parents watch your every move? Were you allowed to bike to a neighbor's house or even play outside without adult supervision? If something didn't go your way at school or on a sports team, did your parents helicopter in to the rescue?

These questions aren't intended to be snarky or judgmental. It's simply a reality, a parenting shift that has deeply impacted this generation, and it has to be faced. If a young adult never learned to get around their own neighborhood unsupervised, never had to deal with a bad grade or tough coach without parental support, how could they be expected to face their own financial futures with the calm and confidence required to step into generous giving at all?

Most impactful of all is this generation's fear of future uncertainty. I believe much of this stems from the twenty-four-hour news cycle we live in. Watch, listen, or read the news at any point during the day, and you'll witness far more negative headlines than positive ones. The world at large seems unstable, and older generations aren't helping Gen Z feel any better about it.

- "What's the world coming to?"
- "I'd be afraid to raise a child in this crazy world."
- "I fear for my grandkids."

Hey, Gramps, that ain't helping. So stop it. (I say that respectfully, of course.)

I get it. We *do* live in a topsy-turvy world, and it's hard to feel like the ground under our feet is firm. But here's some good news from 2 Timothy 1:7: *"God has not given us a spirit of fear and timidity, but of power, love, and self-discipline."*

Fear is a faith issue. If we truly believe in God, the Creator of all things, and we have his spirit inside of us—a spirit of power, love and self-discipline—why would we live in fear?

That doesn't mean God wants us to be reckless, of course—more on that later. But when you're faced by a decision that takes you the way of fear or the way of faith, choose faith. Give abundantly, trusting God with your future as you go.

START SMALL, START SOMEWHERE

Don't let fear stop you from giving. And if you've never had a tithing habit, if you don't know where to start, start *anywhere.*

It's easy to get hung up on details. Should I give my full 10 percent to the church I attend? To this organization or that one? Send monthly checks or make a yearly donation through their handy app? And then, once I find myself earning more than enough and feel a pull to give even more—how do I determine how *much* more?

Just start. Keep it simple. Something is so much better than nothing, and you can always change up your methods once you've gotten in the groove. If you attend a church, give it all to your church to begin with. If you're not a part of a traditional congregation, pick a nonprofit that means something to you. And here's a tip for those having trouble getting into the swing of things at first: automate it.

AUTOMATED GIVING

Think about it. You already have a bunch of monthly subscriptions; even your utility bills are set up with direct deposit. You barely even think about it, probably, but your finances are already automated—just in the wrong direction, toward your own wants and luxuries instead of toward God and the needs of others. Make your giving as convenient and seamless as your streaming subscription, so it's built in to happen whether you're thinking about it or not. You could even set the gifts up to increase by 1 percent or so each year, stretching you toward more and more generous living.

I do have a couple cautions about automated giving, though.

First off, generosity is more than just a choice you make with your money, whether you do it manually and thoughtfully or on autopilot. It's a state of the heart. It's an openness to others and God that bleeds into your daily life beyond the financial sphere. If you're struggling to get in that generous space on a heart level, don't quarantine the idea of generosity to the gifts you can qualify as charitable donations on your tax return. Don't keep it cold, just one piece of your budget, something that never reaches the heart.

Put some cash in your wallet for that guy you always see on the corner. Out to lunch with a friend? Cover their meal for no particular reason. Be generous with your time and talent by volunteering, helping a coworker with their move when you'd far rather be enjoying a good movie on your couch at home, or listening patiently to someone who needs a listener. Try to open yourself up to abundant giving of yourself with your family, your neighbors, and your community at large, and watch how it changes your tithing moving forward. Generosity is a muscle you can exercise and build. It truly is better to give than to receive, and once you start, you'll feel just how true that is.

Second, don't forget the *radical* side of generosity. Automated giving and weekly tithes of 10 percent to the church? Those walk hand in hand with our calling to be good and prudent stewards and managers of God's gifts. Good. We're not meant to be reckless. Those methods of giving are the white button-down, pressed khaki pants, and polished penny loafer version of generosity. Fine and very important, but kind of basic.

Sure, God doesn't call us to be reckless, but he sure doesn't call us to be comfortable either. I believe he wants us to be radical in our giving—not always rational. I'm talking about a neon hair, leather jacket and combat boots style of giving: something a bit wild.

We all need to throw on a pair of holy, ripped-up jeans now and again, and get a little radical.

RADICAL GENEROSITY

That 10 percent rule? It's not the end-all, be-all. It's just a starting point. Especially as you find yourself more and more financially comfortable, your giving should increase accordingly. It should increase *radically*.

Think about all those famous people who consider themselves philanthropists and humanitarian benefactors. They're funding hospitals and research, they're sponsoring children left and right, they're making the news and smiling graciously for the camera.

Then their financial reports come out. Sure, they've given a lot compared to the rest of us; but since they *have* a lot, what they've given turns out to be only about 1 percent of what they *could* give.

Now, I don't want to poo-poo their contributions. But really? You've got all that, and you're only willing to part with a tiny, painless fragment? That's not radical generosity.

Radical generosity is the widow's mite.

If you don't know the story, Jesus once watched the wealthy making their offerings at the temple. Then he saw a poor old widow who offered only two small copper coins. His response? The rich men, he acknowledged, had paid their dues to God, but out of their own abundance, while the widow had offered up the greatest gift of all. She'd given all she had. This is the same Jesus who preaches the truth: "Blessed are the poor, for theirs is the kingdom of God."

Radical generosity looks like this: God first, others second, yourself last. It should be a sacrifice. It should hurt a little, at least at first; it should make you question your own wisdom. Tithing 10 percent is great, but that's just the beginning. Yes, it requires some faith, but once you start doing it and it's built into your budget, it's easy to get too comfortable.

I don't think God ever wants us to get complacent in our giving—with our money, our time, or our talents. Radical generosity will require us to get uncomfortable, but the sacrifice is worth it.

By the way, I'm a firm believer that if you are faithful in your giving, God will provide—just maybe not always the way you'd expect. It could be something as clear as a raise at work, or it could be more subtle: your old car chugs along for a few years longer than you'd expect, or the washer and dryer at home keeps running, or you get an unexpected scholarship for school tuition that would have led to more student loan debt.

The important thing is that there is no formula, no guarantee that if you tithe X amount, God will bless you with Y. God's provision may look totally different than you hope, but guess what? He knows better, and it'll be OK.

Take the leap of faith. Jump into generosity with your whole heart, and just watch what happens.

Focus Questions

1. Just how greedy *are* you? No judgment, but seriously, playing a little game of "Do you have a price?" can reveal a lot about your current relationship with money. How much would someone have to pay you to do something truly terrible, like eat moldy cheese? It sounds silly, but take a minute to think about what levels of anxiety, greed, or dysfunction this question reveals.

2. And speaking of anxiety: what fears (financial or otherwise) are keeping you from giving more freely? Are you letting future uncertainty rob you of present faith?

3. When was the last time you gave in a way that felt sacrificial or radical? How did that stretch or bless you?

Do It Today

1. Do a quick giving audit: What percentage of your income do you currently give away? Where does that money go, and is it consistent and planned or infrequent and sporadic?

2. Choose one way to upgrade your giving:
   - Start tithing 10 percent if you aren't yet.
   - Automate your giving.
   - Try to add one spontaneous moment of generosity per week (pay for someone's meal, give something away, etc.).
   - Increase your giving (if it's already a consistent habit) by at least 1 percent each year, starting today.

Chapter 9

BUILDING WEALTH WISELY

Gain all you can, save all you can, give all you can.

—JOHN WESLEY

INVESTING: AN ACT OF GREED?

So, we've talked about contentment, generosity, stewardship, all the things. At this point, when you hear the word *investing*, you might have a gut reaction of "Huh—trying to build up wealth? Doesn't sound very stewardship-y." I don't blame you for thinking that way.

Though the love of money is the root of all evil, money itself certainly ain't. So, is seeking wealth a sin? It depends on your motives. Ask God to check your heart. If you're in it for greed, status, all the worldly things we've spent so much time discussing, then yeah. That's a no-go.

But if your motives have to do with hard work, with generosity, with being able to have a big, positive impact on the world and people around you? Then I'd say you've got nothing to worry about.

What does wise, stewardship-minded wealth-building really look like, then? It might seem like an intimidating process to consider, and I do encourage you to read slowly because this can feel like a lot when you first dive in. My hope for you is that this chapter will supply you with the simple, practical guidance and tips you need to get started.

BEFORE YOU BEGIN: LAYING THE FOUNDATION

I'm sorry: we haven't even begun to talk about investing, but I'd be remiss in my duties as a financial advisor if I didn't start with a caveat.

I'm about to tell you how important it is to begin investing as early as humanly possible, but *it is possible to start too soon*. When I meet with young clients, these are the steps I encourage them to be sure to take before even *thinking* about wider investment plans:

- **Set up an emergency fund**. That means having three to six months of your total living expenses set aside. Why? Because life happens. Things like a job loss, medical bills, or car repairs. Without a safety net, you'll be forced to rely on credit cards, personal loans, or family and friends. (Did you know? Nearly 60 percent of Americans can't cover a $1,000 emergency.)[29]

- **Erase your consumer debt**. Don't start investing until that credit card is paid off. Now, there's some wiggle room here. I firmly advise you not to start investing while you have *credit card debt*, specifically, but do you need to wait until your mortgage has been paid? Or your auto loan, if you're unfortunate enough to have one, or your student debt? There's more room for interpretation there. Auto loans and student debts generally carry much lower interest rates than credit cards do. That's why the essential debt to wipe out, in my book, is credit card debt: don't turn your eyes to investing until that's been totally taken care of. With 20+ percent interest rates on credit cards (double the average return of the stock market), it's counterproductive to invest while carrying credit card debt. So paying it off might actually be your best investment.

- **Build some margin**. Once you have an emergency fund and no credit card debt, take some time to breathe and make sure you have surplus funds available *before* turning your attention to making serious investments.

One final note: remember that 10/10/80 rule? The 10 percent suggested starting point for savings refers to the savings you send into your long-term, set-it-and-forget-it *retirement funds*. Your monthly 10 percent savings contribution should start going toward your retirement ASAP (after you get your emergency fund set, of course).

We'll dive into the how-tos and recommendations for building that retirement fund shortly, but I wanted to be clear that anything more complex than a simple retirement saving plan *should not be attempted* before you are sure you have the time and extra funds to look beyond that baseline 10 percent. (And, if you do reach the point of wanting to create a more customized investing strategy, that'd be the time to seek the advice of a CERTIFIED FINANCIAL PLANNER™ who can take you beyond the basics laid out in this chapter.)

OK. Got all that? An emergency fund, no credit card debt, a little bit of margin, the reminder to prioritize a retirement fund. *Now* we're ready to dig in.

WHY **SHOULD** YOU INVEST? ISN'T PLAIN OLD SAVING ENOUGH?

Before we talk strategy, let's make sure you're crystal clear on what investing even *is*—and how it's different from saving.

Think of saving like putting money in a piggy bank: it's low-risk and feels "safe," but it grows very slowly. In fact, if your savings account is earning 1 percent interest while inflation rises at 2 percent, you're actually *losing* money over time, even though the dollar amount looks the same. As an illustration, you could gather up enough money to buy a house and bury it in the backyard for safekeeping, but when you pull it out fifty years later, all it'll buy you is a pound of potatoes. (I'm exaggerating, but you get the picture.)

Investing, on the other hand, puts your money to work through the ownership of assets that grow in value or produce income for you over time. It involves a bit of risk compared to a simple savings account, sure. But the long-term reward is much greater.

You might be thinking, *OK, saving grows slowly, and investing grows faster, but so what? Retirement is practically a lifetime away. I don't need to think about it yet.*

Your future self is going to need to eat, pay bills, and live life. And thanks to inflation, everything will be more expensive. A person who spends $10,000 a year on groceries today could be spending over $32,000 a year by the time they retire. (Like I said, I was exaggerating about that pound of potatoes, but maybe not by much.) Multiply that by the twenty or thirty years you'll spend as a retired person. You're looking at hundreds of thousands of dollars just for food.

And that's before you factor in housing, healthcare, and everyday life. Social Security, by the way, only replaces about 40 percent of the average income now, and with people living longer and the system under strain, you can't count on it to cover you. Do you want to be able to be generous with your time and resources once you have grandkids, to volunteer and serve stress-free, or spend your later years worrying about money?

Even small, regular investments can snowball into something significant. Don't wait until it's urgent. The earlier you start, the better off you'll be.

START EARLY, START SMALL, START SIMPLE

That's really the biggest piece of investing advice I can give you: *start as early as you can.* The single biggest advantage you have in investing is time.

I like to illustrate why an early start is important using a couple book characters from my childhood: P. D. Eastman's Fred and Ted. Let's say Fred and Ted are the exact same age and hold similar jobs that make a similar amount: around $50,000 per year. Both of them start investing 10 percent of their annual paycheck ($5,000 per year) at a modest 6 percent per year return on their investments.

But here's the thing: Fred started when he was twenty-two, so by the time he hits his sixties, he's been investing for forty years. Ted, on the other hand, didn't get started till he was thirty-two, and winds up with a thirty-year investing history when it comes time to retire. When both Fred and Ted are sixty-two, early-bird Fred will have $773,808, and procrastinator Ted will have $378,516. Fred has *nearly twice as much* saved as Ted, even though he only invested a total of $50,000 more than Ted overall. Those ten extra years of investing made a massive, massive difference.

Fred & Ted Comparison Charts

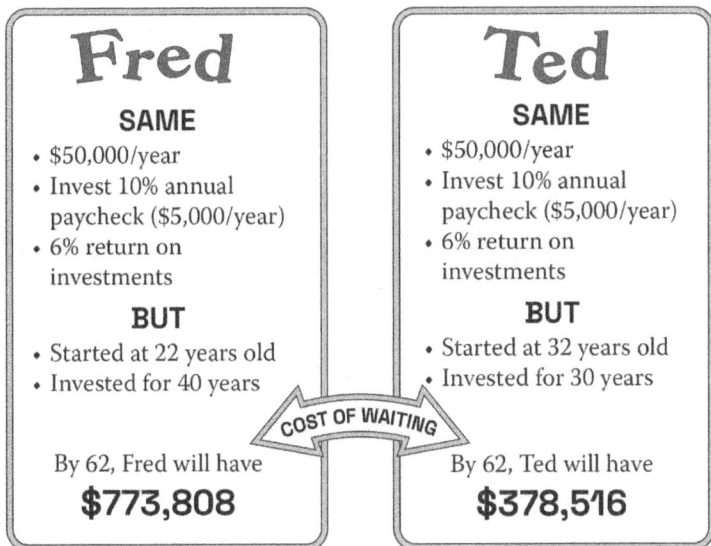

Fred

SAME

- $50,000/year
- Invest 10% annual paycheck ($5,000/year)
- 6% return on investments

BUT

- Started at 22 years old
- Invested for 40 years

By 62, Fred will have

$773,808

Ted

SAME

- $50,000/year
- Invest 10% annual paycheck ($5,000/year)
- 6% return on investments

BUT

- Started at 32 years old
- Invested for 30 years

By 62, Ted will have

$378,516

COST OF WAITING

So, again, start as early as you can.

Many people think they don't have enough money to start investing, but even beginning with very small increments can make a big difference. What about a dollar a day? Thirty dollars per month? Sounds doable, right? I promise you that even that small amount will have a huge impact, given time.

But let's even go a little further here: a cup of coffee from Starbucks costs five dollars, and it goes in and out of you in less than an hour. So imagine you cut that habit and invest five dollars a day instead.

Let me crunch *those* numbers for you.

If you invested five dollars a day for ten years and earned a conservative 6 percent annually, you'd have nearly $25,000 in the end. Extend that timeline to forty years, and the results are staggering: $291,570 at that conservative 6 percent—or close to $1,000,000 if your investments average 10 percent annually, like the historical performance of the S&P 500.

S&P 500: Standard and Poor's 500 is a stock market index tracking the stock performance of five hundred leading US companies. Historically, it has averaged about 10 percent annually, though returns vary year to year. (Disclaimer: of course, although widely referenced and used for planning purposes, past performance is not necessarily a guarantee of future performance.)

The point of all this math is to show you that your greatest advantage is time. Time is what makes the magic of *compound interest* happen (more on that below). Time is your greatest asset, and this is true in both investing and life.

A REMINDER: COMPOUND INTEREST

We briefly talked about compound interest back in our chapter on debt—remember how credit card debt has that nasty habit of snowballing? You borrow a hundred dollars, but you're paying 25 percent interest on the loan. So that owed balance jumps to $125, then $156.25, then just keeps growing—because you're not just paying interest on the original amount. You're paying interest on the interest.

Compound interest plays a role in your investments, too, but this time, it acts in your favor.

Instead of your debt snowballing out of control, your *wealth* starts snowballing upward. Each dollar you invest earns a little interest, and then that interest starts earning interest... and then *that* interest starts earning interest. At first, the growth feels small and slow, but it accelerates over time.

It's kind of like bamboo: it grows slowly, almost invisibly, for years. Then suddenly, boom. It shoots up feet at a time. That's how compound interest works, and the sooner you begin, the sooner that growth can take off.

A Useful Shortcut: The Rule of 72

To estimate how long it will take for your investment to double, divide seventy-two by the expected interest rate (or growth rate/rate of return). For example:

Earning 6 percent annually? Your money will double in about twelve years (72 ÷ 6).

Earning 2 percent in a savings account? That's thirty-six years to double (72 ÷ 2).

But if you're paying 20 percent interest on a credit card? Your *debt* doubles in just 3.6 years (72 ÷ 20).>

This is why I keep emphasizing an early start and consistency. You don't need a huge amount of money to begin. Just $30 a month—a dollar a day—can grow into something meaningful over time. The real key isn't timing the market; it's time *in* the market.

One last illustration to really bring the power of compound interest home for you.

Have you ever played "Would you rather?" This has become a favorite dinner game in our family. My kids love it: "Would you rather be as fast as a cheetah or as strong as a gorilla?"

Then my wife joins in: "Would you rather eat a pickle-flavored cupcake or a bacon-flavored milkshake?"

Then it's my turn: "Would you rather have $1 million today or a penny that doubles every day for a month?"

Huh? Dad's trying to trick us into doing money math again. Fun over.

The thing is, though, I do have a point with that question. *That doubling penny turns into over $5 million after thirty days.* Why? Good old compound interest. Most of the growth happens in the last few days. That's the power of starting early and giving your money time to work.

Penny Doubled Chart, 30 Days

Day	Amount ($)	Day	Amount ($)
1	$0.01	16	$327.68
2	$0.02	17	$655.36
3	$0.04	18	$1,310.72
4	$0.08	19	$2,621.44
5	$0.16	20	$5,242.88
6	$0.32	21	$10,485.76
7	$0.64	22	$20,971.52
8	$1.28	23	$41,943.04
9	$2.56	24	$83,886.08
10	$5.12	25	$167,772.16
11	$10.24	26	$335,544.32
12	$20.48	27	$671,088.64
13	$40.96	28	$1,342,177.28
14	$81.92	29	$2,684,354.56
15	$163.84	30	$5,368,709.12

DECISION TIME: TOOLS AND WISE STRATEGIES

OK. You've got a solid understanding of the prerequisites (emergency fund, no credit card debt, and so on). You know the difference between saving and investing; you understand why it's so important to get started as early as you can, even if you have to start small, and you get how compound interest works. You're ready to invest. So, where do you start?

In the sections that follow, I'm going to break down the tools and strategies for you:

1. The two main kinds of investment accounts.
2. The main investment types.
3. A couple strategies I highly recommend using as you get started.

TYPES OF INVESTMENT ACCOUNTS

Let's start with where your investments actually go. You'll need an account—kind of like the bucket that holds your money as it grows. There are two main types to consider: retirement accounts and brokerage accounts.

First up, we've got retirement accounts. These guys are built for the long haul. You know how I feel about them: if there's one place to begin, it's here. They come with powerful tax advantages to reward long-term investing, and the goal is in the name.

If your job offers a 401(k) *with a match*, definitely grab it—that's free money. It's an automatic 100 percent return on whatever you contribute up to the match limit. If they'll match 3 percent of your salary, at *least* contribute that much. Then, if you can do more, don't stop there. Your employer's match should just be the icing on the cake. Save as much as you can *yourself*, and consider the match amount a nice bonus. So many people just lean on the existence of their employer retirement account without even paying attention to how much is going into it. Stay thoughtful. Stay aware.

And if your employer doesn't offer a 401(k), look into opening an IRA (Individual Retirement Account). You've got two main options:

- **Traditional IRA:** You don't pay taxes on the money you contribute now, but you will when you take it out later. That means you save on your taxes *today*. This helps lower your current taxable income.
- **Roth IRA:** You don't get the tax savings today, but your money grows tax-free and you can take it out tax-free in retirement. Often better for younger investors because you're likely in a lower tax bracket (making less money) now than you will be when you're older. Bonus: you can withdraw your contributions, though not the interest they've earned, at any time without penalty (and there are exceptions that allow you to withdraw both your contributions *and* their earnings penalty-free)—but try to resist the urge to access any of it prior to retirement.

So, that's the low-down on retirement accounts. *That's where you'll start.*

Once you've set up your retirement contributions through a 401(k) or an IRA, or if you find you want more flexibility, *then* you can consider opening a brokerage account. Think of it as a general-purpose investing account.

With brokerage accounts, you can buy and sell investments at any time, and there's no early withdrawal penalty. The catch? You'll owe taxes on any profits, dividends, or interest. And the real danger here is how easy it is to dip into brokerage funds when they're not earmarked for retirement. So, if you do go this route, *stay disciplined.*

A Tip for Brokerage Accounts

If you sell an investment after holding it for more than a year, you'll pay a lower tax rate. But if you sell it sooner, your profits get taxed like regular income. Some dividends are taxed at lower rates, too. You can choose to reinvest those earnings automatically, which helps your money grow faster over time.

PICK YOUR INVESTMENTS

Now that you've chosen your bucket, or type of investment account, let's talk about what goes *inside* it.

What kind of investments do you want to tackle? Here's the basic breakdown of your options:

- **Stocks:** You own a piece of a company by buying shares (of stock). Higher risk, but higher potential growth.
- **Bonds:** When you purchase bonds, you're essentially lending money to governments or companies who then pay you interest in return. Generally less risky than stocks, but typically deliver lower returns.
- **ETFs/Index Funds:** A bundle of stocks or bonds that track the market (such as the S&P 500 or aggregate bond index)—great for beginners because it spreads the risk out among hundreds of investments. (This is called diversification.)

+ **Real Estate:** Long-term investment through property. Harder to start (you typically need to be able to put a lot of money down for it to pay off), but theoretically possible.

> **Exchange-traded funds (ETFs):** Bundles of diversified investments that grow with the market. By automatically spreading your money across multiple companies in the market, you don't have to worry if just one of them individually (as one five hundredth of your total investment) goes belly-up.

Remember: whichever option you choose, you shouldn't need thousands to get started. Apps today let you invest with just five dollars—and give you the option to spread your money across various investments to lower your risk.

RECOMMENDED STRATEGIES: DOLLAR-COST AVERAGING AND AUTOMATION

Here's one strategy I strongly recommend, especially when you're starting out: dollar-cost averaging (or DCA for short).

Let's say you commit to putting fifty dollars a month toward buying shares in a given company. One month, the market is up, so each share costs more, and your fifty dollars buys you *fewer shares*. The next month, the market dips, and you buy more shares with that same fifty dollars. In the end, this strategy smooths out the ups and downs. You're not biting your nails, trying to guess when to "buy low" or "sell high"—you're just trusting the process and letting your strategy do the work for you.

Over time, like the tortoise in the old fable, and regardless of the market's swings, you *will* end up with a fund that snowballs into something significant. And you'll have done it using a steady, stress-free strategy that kept your emotions and any fearful or greedy impulses out of the equation.

> **Dollar-cost averaging (DCA):** The practice of investing the same amount of money in the same way at a regular interval, no matter what.

Here's another simple strategy to consider: automation. Treat your investment contributions like any old subscription. Just like your giving, just like your streaming services, you can automate your contributions to your 401(k), IRA, or brokerage account. That way, you're building wealth without even thinking about it. You can just set it and forget it.

It's one of the smartest moves you can make, and it'll be worth it in the long run.

A FEW WORDS OF CAUTION

As you get started in your investing, I have to spend the next few sections of this chapter on some warnings. Not super fun, I know, but this is what's ahead:

1. As you earn more, don't spend more. *Invest* more instead.
2. The stock market is not a casino.
3. Trading is *not* the same as investing (spoiler: it's investing's evil cousin and should be avoided, IMHO).

So let's dive into the "don'ts," shall we?

AVOID LIFESTYLE CREEP
(INVESTMENT-FOCUSED REMIX)

As your income grows, so does the temptation to upgrade your lifestyle—nicer car, bigger house, trendier clothes. But if you're always upgrading, you'll always feel broke, even as you earn more.

Instead of *spending* every extra dollar, make a habit of *investing* your raises and bonuses first. A simple rule is to put at least half of every raise into savings or investments. Many people spend their bonus money before it even hits their account, like in *National Lampoon's Christmas Vacation*—Clark was banking on that bonus to cover his family's expenses, and the disappointment hit hard. Another way to avoid that trap, besides just investing half of every raise or bonus, is to automatically increase your 401(k) or retirement contributions by 1–2 percent each year. You won't miss the money, and your future self will thank you. Remember: thirty years from now, you won't be looking back and wishing you'd bought more clothes; you'll be wishing you'd planned better.

THE STOCK MARKET IS NOT A CASINO

My next word of warning is a simple reminder that your investment account is not a slot machine.

When you buy a stock, you're not rolling dice—you're buying a piece of a real company that makes things, employs people, and generates profit. You're not betting on luck; you're building long-term value.

Yes, the market goes up and down. That's normal. A dip doesn't mean the system is broken, just like a rainy day doesn't mean the sky is falling. Selling during a dip is like selling your house because Zillow says it dropped in value for a month. During COVID's early days in 2020, the stock market *did* drop nearly 30 percent in a month. It felt like the world was ending. But by late March—while headlines were still grim—the market had already started to recover.

That's the thing: the market and the economy don't move at the same pace. Often, by the time things *feel* safe, the market rebound has already happened. Timing the market rarely works, but consistent investment does the trick.

That said, of course, you can't throw your money into just anything and hope for the best, come what may. Understand the balance of risk and reward. Higher potential returns usually come with higher risk, which is where diversification helps. Spreading your money across different investments, paired with strategies like dollar-cost averaging, helps keep things balanced.

Don't be fearful, but be wise. Keep emotion out of it as much as you can. And don't fall for the hype online. Just because someone made quick money on crypto or meme stocks doesn't mean you should try it. Most of those stories skip over the losses.

Meme stock: A stock that gets popular with retail traders thanks to social media; characterized by huge price swings, a large volume of trading, big investors betting **against** the company, and smaller investors betting **on** the company.

TRADING

Speaking of which, here's your third word of caution: investing is *not* the same thing as trading.

Investing means buying something like Apple stock because you believe in the company's long-term growth. Trading, on the other hand, is trying to buy low and sell high over and over again. It's high-risk, high-stress, and highly emotional. While investing can be kept rational with habits like automation and dollar-cost averaging, trading often turns into a tug-of-war between fear and greed. Even worse, statistically, most traders lose money. (Some estimates say 80–90 percent.) When you're trading instead of investing, the odds aren't in your favor.

Take Apple during COVID. In March 2020, the stock dropped nearly 30 percent, not because Apple was failing but because everyone was panicking. A trader might have sold in fear. But by the end of 2021, Apple's stock had more than doubled. Then came inflation in 2022, and it dropped again. Trying to time every rise and fall? Nearly impossible.

There's a saying I like: "Your money is like a bar of soap—the more you handle it, the less you'll have."[30] In the past, investors had to call a broker to make trades, creating a natural pause, a chance to think. Now, apps gamify trading, and you can buy and sell with a quick tap of the finger. That's not investing. It's gambling.

Even legendary traders haven't escaped the dangers. Jesse Livermore, the OG trader, made over $100 million by shorting the market in 1929 (over $1.5 billion today). Like a poker player cashing in at the blackjack table, Livermore felt invincible—until he wasn't. He spent the rest of his life chasing that one big win, riding a roller coaster of emotions and losses until he tragically took his own life in 1940. Nearly a hundred years later, the cycle continues.

In 2020 and 2021, pandemic boredom, stimulus checks, and free trading apps created a new wave of day traders. Robinhood made it feel like anyone could strike gold. GameStop became the meme stock of the movement—fueled by Reddit and a guy named Roaring Kitty. For a moment, it felt like David was beating Goliath.

But for most people, the story didn't end in victory. A few fast wins turned into losses, maxed-out credit cards, and a sinking feeling of "What just happened?" They doubled down, ignored logic, and kept going, hoping to break even. What started as a fun experiment with a "stimmy check" became a financial mess.

(By the way, if that was you, don't panic. This isn't the end of your story. You're not a failure—you just paid a "dumb tax," as some call it. Consider it tuition for your real-world finance degree. Learn from it. Reset. You're young, and the best time to rebuild is now.)

By the Way: A Word About Gambling

As a kid, my dad and I would swing by the local convenience store for one of two essentials—either the early '90's version of a protein shake (you know, a Yoo-Hoo) or a pouch of grape-flavored Big League Chew. But there was something else in that store that caught my attention. It had flashing lights, arcade-like buttons, and a red cushioned stool. A poker machine.

Back in the early '90s, you didn't need to travel to Vegas to gamble; you could do it right next to the Slushie machine. I remember watching grown men stop in on their way home from work—wallets full after payday, tired, stressed, and maybe just grabbing a loaf of bread for dinner. But instead of going straight to the bread aisle, they'd sit down at that machine.

I can still picture one of them: a father of three, white-knuckling the seat. He loses a few games, then gets a small win. Not enough to break even, but enough to pull him deeper in. He plays again. And again. Two hours later, the loaf of bread is forgotten. So is the paycheck.

Those machines are illegal in most gas stations now, but gambling isn't. Scratch-offs and state lotteries have filled the gap, labeled "education lotteries" to ease the conscience. The odds of winning are about one in three hundred million. You're more likely to become president or get crushed by a vending machine than win the jackpot. But at least it's "for the kids," right?

The truth is that gambling has gotten more accessible than ever. All you need is a phone, and you can even link your credit card straight to an app. It's highly addictive, and we've rebranded it. It's not "gambling" anymore. That word feels shady. Now it's called "betting." That sounds strategic.

Take fantasy football, for example. What started as a fun hobby—drafting real players to build your dream team—has turned into a gateway drug for many. A guy joins a casual league with friends, gets hooked, does research, watches games obsessively. Next season, there's a buy-in. Then he buys a streaming pass so he can watch every game. Before long, he isn't just playing football. He's in a fantasy hockey league, and he's never even skated.

I had my own version of this in college. A friend told me about a site where you started with one cent to bet on games. I was a baseball fan, so that's what I picked. At first, it was fun. Then baseball wasn't enough. One night, I stayed up late watching an NHL game I'd bet twelve cents on—twelve cents. I couldn't tell you who was playing or if I won, but I remember the rush. That was the moment I realized I couldn't gamble on sports. Not even a penny. If I wanted to enjoy the game, I had to leave money out of it.

Fantasy sports may seem harmless, but they're often a stepping stone to more destructive habits. Now, you can't watch a game without seeing ads for sports betting apps. It's big business. ESPN even has its own betting platform. Leagues like the NBA are cashing in, too, partnering with sportsbooks to monetize the madness.

And if you're not into traditional sports, there's always esports. Video game competitions have exploded. Gamers go head-to-head on screens while millions watch—and bet—on the outcome. My brother and I used to battle it out on the original Nintendo with games like "Mike Tyson's Punch-Out!" Recently, he texted me a meme comparing Glass Joe from the game to Jake Paul before his fight with Tyson. Apparently, more than sixty million people watched it. Tyson made $20 million. Paul made $40 million. Why'd they fight? Cue ABBA: "Money, money, money..."

Side note: ABBA's name comes from the first initials of its four members—Agnetha, Björn, Benny, and Anni-Frid, and they had to negotiate with a Swedish fish-canning company called Abba to use the name. But more importantly, in Aramaic, Abba means "father." It's how Jesus addressed God in the garden, full of intimacy and trust:

- Mark 14:36 – *"Abba, Father, all things are possible for You. Take this cup away from Me; nevertheless, not what I will, but what You will."*
- Romans 8:15 – *"You received the Spirit of adoption by whom we cry out, 'Abba, Father.'"*
- Galatians 4:6 – *"Because you are sons, God has sent forth the Spirit of His Son into your hearts, crying out, 'Abba, Father!'"*

That kind of connection puts our earthly obsessions in perspective.

Whether it's poker machines, fantasy leagues, and twelve-cent NHL bets or trading and meme stocks, the highs never last. But our Father—our Abba—offers something real. Something lasting. Something better.

A FINAL ENCOURAGEMENT: DON'T FORGET TO INVEST IN YOURSELF

OK. Whew. That was a lot. I hope you're underlining and dog-earing the heck out of this chapter so you can come back because I know there's tons here to digest in one go. Remember: you can educate yourself all you want, but at the end of the day, you *may* also find you need a financial professional walking alongside you through the complexity.

Let's close out this chapter with an important reminder, and an encouragement.

Investing in the market is important, sure. I just spent an info-packed chapter expounding on why. And obviously, investing in the kingdom matters more than anything else, but outside of that? The next-best investment you can make is probably in *yourself*.

That includes your skills, your mindset, and your personal growth. It also means investing in your career path. We talk a lot about spending habits, but you can only cut so much, and working to increase your income can make more of a difference in your financial margin than all the budget-trimming in the world.

Investing in yourself doesn't mean neglecting generosity or investing in kingdom work but rather recognizing that your capacity to give and serve expands as you grow. Consider allocating 3–5 percent of your income to self-development. Even 1 percent is a great start.

That might look like reading one book a month on personal finance, investing, or leadership. It could mean taking online courses or getting certifications that enhance your career. Maybe it's hiring a coach, attending networking events, or listening to business and finance podcasts during your commute. (Just be careful—algorithms can lead you down a get-rich-quick rabbit hole if you're not discerning.)

Think of yourself like a stock: your value increases as you develop your skills and mindset. A better skillset means better opportunities, higher income, and more freedom. Ever known someone who excelled early in life but plateaued because they didn't continue to grow? The best athletes and leaders have coaches. Talent × effort = skill. Skill × effort = achievement (thanks to Angela Duckworth's *Grit* for that formula).

In investing *and* in self-development, growth requires intentionality and consistency. I pray you'll commit to both. The future you're building is worth it.

Focus Questions

1. What's your relationship with time when it comes to money? Do you think in short-term wins or long-term growth?
2. What are your motivations for building wealth? Are they rooted in security, generosity, ego, fear, or purpose?
3. What is your plan for financial self-education? How are you investing in your own growth as a steward, a professional, and a giver?

Do It Today

1. Assess your foundation. Do you have an emergency fund? How much credit card debt are you in? Make a plan to tackle one or the other through automated monthly contributions or extra payments starting today.

2. Do you have a retirement account? If you don't have one, Google "how to open a Roth IRA" and take fifteen minutes to start the process with a trusted platform. If you already have one, log in and check your contribution rate. Bump it up by 1 percent. And remember: if your company offers a 401k match, take advantage of it and sign up!

Part 4

THE PATH FORWARD
BEGINS NOW

Chapter 10

MY HOPES FOR YOU

Finally, brothers and sisters, whatever is true, whatever is noble, whatever is right, whatever is pure, whatever is lovely, whatever is admirable— if anything is excellent or praiseworthy—think about such things.

—PHILIPPIANS 4:8

KISS (KEEP IT SIMPLE, ~~STUPID~~ STEWARD)

Well, my friends, that's the book. I'm so grateful you joined me for this ride, this deep exploration of what it looks like to handle money God's way in a wild world. We've discussed a lot in the previous chapters, from stewardship to how our friends impact our money decisions to the basics of investing. So much of what is written in these pages was put together to help you think about the "why" behind your money decisions: because if you know and understand that "why" (stewardship of all you have for God's glory and the service of others) it will be much easier to implement and sustain the "how" and the "what" (wise, judicious decisions around career, time management, spending, giving, and so much more).

One of my favorite verses in the Bible is Romans 12:2. It was an often-quoted passage of Scripture at my alma mater, Southern Wesleyan University, and it is one that I regularly refer back to even today. Here's what it says: "Do not conform to the pattern of this world, but be transformed by the renewing of your mind. Then you will be able to test and approve what God's will is—his good, pleasing and perfect will." Take a moment to just breathe that one in, settling into a new acceptance and understanding of who you are: a steward of God's good gifts, shaped by God's norms and desires, *not* the meaningless scrabbling and comparison the world wants you to chase.

The world puts self at the center, but as followers of Jesus, God should replace self at the center of our lives. I pray you'll step out into your financial journey—and your growth and faith journey, in general—empowered to do just that.

In closing, I wanted to give you a few practical, summative steps. Honestly, I was hesitant to include this list because I didn't want to water down the significance of the bigger picture we've spent so much time discussing. But I also appreciate the importance and convenience of having practical action steps that can be implemented in your daily lives. Maybe this list is something you can copy down and tack on your mirror or on your desk for a quick reminder each day, a handy little breakdown to remind you of what really matters as you work, serve, spend, and save every day.

So here are ten simple and timeless money concepts, all biblically based, that can carry you through a life filled with the joy and freedom that good stewardship provides:

1. **Live Below Your Means**: Spend less than you earn to create financial margin. This discipline allows you to save, give, and avoid the stress of overspending (Proverbs 21:20).
2. **Budget Wisely with the 10/10/80 Method**: Allocate 10 percent of your income to giving, 10 percent to savings, and 80 percent to spending. As your income grows over time, resist lifestyle creep by increasing your giving and saving percentages while reducing your spending percentage. Plan thoughtfully, but hold your plans loosely, trusting God's provision (Proverbs 16:9).
3. **Avoid Debt**: Borrow sparingly, if at all, and prioritize paying off debts quickly. Debt can enslave you, limiting your ability to serve God freely (Proverbs 22:7).

4. **Guard Against Greed**: Pursue contentment over wealth. True riches come from a heart aligned with God's purposes, not the pursuit of more (1 Timothy 6:6–10).
5. **Choose Relationships Wisely**: Surround yourself with friends and, if you marry, a spouse who shares your values of stewardship and faith. Godly companions sharpen your decisions (Proverbs 13:20).
6. **Work Diligently for God (Audience of One)**: Use your talents faithfully, working hard as unto the Lord, not for human approval. Your effort honors God and builds a legacy (Colossians 3:23–24).
7. **Give Generously and Cheerfully**: Share your resources with a joyful heart, trusting God to multiply your gifts for his kingdom (2 Corinthians 9:7).
8. **Stop Comparing (Play your Own Game)**: Focus on your unique calling and financial journey. Comparison breeds discontentment, while gratitude fosters peace (Galatians 6:4–5).
9. **Remember God Owns It All**: You are a steward, not an owner, of the resources God entrusts to you. Manage them wisely to honor him (Psalm 24:1).
10. **Know Whose You Are**: Your identity is in Christ, not your wealth or possessions. Anchor your heart in God's love and faithfulness (1 Peter 2:9).

By embracing these principles, you can experience the joy and freedom of stewarding God's resources well, living a life that reflects his glory.

MY PRAYER FOR
YOUR JOURNEY AHEAD

Lord God,

Thank you for walking with us through these pages, through the questions and convictions, hard truths, and fresh hope. You are the giver of every good gift—time, talents, treasure—and our deepest prayer is to steward them well.

For the person holding this book, standing on the edge of financial and life choices, both big and small, I pray for clarity, for faith, and for the courage of a honey badger. Give them eyes to see what truly matters, ears to hear your voice above the noise, and a heart that beats in rhythm with yours. Teach them to plan boldly, give joyfully, and work faithfully.

When the world pushes greed, ego, and competition, remind them that their worth is not in their wallets but in being your beloved and trusted servants. When they feel behind or unsure, anchor them in the truth that it's never too late to start walking in wisdom.

Bless their efforts. Multiply what's surrendered. Lead them into generosity that changes lives—including their own.

May they live with open hands, grateful hearts, and an eternal perspective.

In Jesus's name,
Amen.

ACKNOWLEDGMENTS

This book reflects the profound impact of those who've shaped my path.

My dad, Tim, you showed me true dedication, always making time after long workdays to practice sports with me outside.

My mom, Karen, you kept me anchored in faith through church and believed in my potential, even when risks loomed large.

My brother, Brandon, your big brotherly love, mixed with relentless sarcasm and lighthearted torture, kept me humble and grounded.

Professor Bowen, you showed me how to align work with faith, inspiring me to live with purpose. Professor Frazier, your lesson on compound interest in my first class was a revelation, and cofounding the investment club together shaped my journey.

To Greg, my mentor, your texts, calls, and coffee shop talks have been a lifeline—your understanding means the world.

Together, your support made this book possible, and I'm forever grateful.

ABOUT THE AUTHOR

KYLE BLACKWELL is a husband and father whose faith shapes how he sees money, work, and the decisions that build a life. He became interested in investing early on—curious about how businesses grow and how ordinary people can take part. He is also a CERTIFIED FINANCIAL PLANNER™, a role that has allowed him to walk with people through their most important financial decisions.

He started his career by knocking on doors, introducing himself one conversation at a time. He learned that most people don't need complexity. They need clarity and someone willing to listen. After more than a decade in the industry, he launched his own advisory practice, which was later acquired. His work has been noted by Forbes and InvestmentNews, but the real measure has always been the trust people placed in him.

Along the way, Kyle noticed a gap. Young adults weren't failing because they lacked talent or effort. They were making their first financial decisions surrounded by noise but short on wisdom—left to sort through conflicting voices with no reliable framework to guide them. The Purpose Path grew out of that gap. It includes *Purpose in Every Paycheck,* the Purpose Playbook course, and the Purpose Planner app—tools designed to equip young adults with confidence and direction as they navigate money for the first time.

Kyle lives in Clemson, South Carolina, with his wife and their two children. Much of what he believes about stewardship and purpose has been shaped by the ordinary moments of family life—conversations and questions that quietly clarify what truly matters.

You can find him at **KyleBlackwell.com.**

ENDNOTES

1. Empower, Secret to Success study, 2024. https://www.empower.com/the-currency/money/secret-success-research.

2. Social Security Administration, National Average Wage Index, https://www.ssa.gov/oact/cola/AWI.html.

3. Amanda Amos and Margaretha Haglund, "From Social Taboo to 'Torch of Freedom': The Marketing of Cigarettes to Women," Tobacco Control 9 No. 1 (2000): 4, https://www.jstor.org.proxy.bib.uottawa.ca/stable/20207720?seq=1#page_scan_tab_contents.

4. "Household Debt and Credit Report, Q4 2024," Federal Reserve Bank of New York, accessed April 23, 2025, https://www.newyorkfed.org/microeconomics/hhdc.

5. "Stress in America 2023: A Nation Recovering from Collective Trauma," American Psychological Association, November 2023, accessed April 23, 2025, https://www.apa.org/news/press/releases/stress/2023/collective-trauma-recovery.

6. Cary Schmidt, *Stop Trying* (Moody Publishers, 2021), 20.

7. Schmidt, Stop Trying, chap. 8.

8. "Just Tickled," People, January 13, 1997, accessed April 23, 2025.

9. Leon Festinger, "A Theory of Social Comparison Processes" (1954), retrieved April 23, 2025, from hum.sagepub.com

10. Quote attributed to Bernard Meltzer.

11. Walter Mischel and Ebbe B. Ebbesen, Ebbe B., "Attention in delay of gratification," Journal of Personality and Social Psychology 16, No. 2 (1970): 329–337.

12. John Piper, *Don't Waste Your Life* (Crossway: 2003), 45–46.

13. "Regrets of the Dying," bronnieware.com, accessed April 23, 2025.

14. Suzy Welch, *10-10-10: A Life-Transforming Idea* (Scribner: 2009).

15. Martin Luther King Jr., "What Is Your Life's Blueprint?" (speech, Barratt Junior High School, Philadelphia, PA, October 26, 1967).

16. "Wasting Time At Work Statistics: How & Why We Do It + Ways to Prevent It in 2024," TeamStage, accessed April 23, 2025, https://teamstage.io/wasting-time-at-work-statistics/.

17. "Introducing the Eisenhower Matrix," Eisenhower, accessed April 23, 2025, https://www.eisenhower.me/eisenhower-matrix/.

18. James Clear, *Atomic Habits* (Avery, 2018), 74.

19. Hannah Nowack, "How Much Does the Average Wedding Cost, According to Data?" The Knot, updated February 26, 2025, https://www.theknot.com/content/average-wedding-cost.

20. Henry Cloud, *Necessary Endings: The Employees, Businesses, and Relationships That All of Us Have to Give Up in Order to Move Forward* (Harper Business, 2011).

21. Chart from pagetear.com in a social post by @heyblake on X, "Cognitive Bias."

22. Genesis 25:29–34.

23. Janet Lowe, *Warren Buffett Speaks* (Wiley, 1997), 143.

24. Erin Hurd, "Does Using a Credit Card Make You Spend More Money?" Nerd Wallet, updated May 28, 2024, accessed April 23, 2025, https://www.nerdwallet.com/article/credit-cards/credit-cards-make-you-spend-more.

25. Franck, Thomas. "College Tuition Has Increased 1,200% Since 1980," *CNBC*, August 15, 2022, https://www.cnbc.com/2022/08/15/college-tuition-has-increased-1200percent-since-1980.html.

26. Taylor Covington, "Supersized: Americans Are Living in Bigger Houses With Fewer People," The Zebra, May 15, 2024, https://www.thezebra.com/resources/home/median-home-size-in-us/.

27. Eric Foley, "Churchgoers Less Generous Today Than During the Great Depression," Do the Word, August 9, 2010, https://dotheword.org/2010/08/09/churchgoers-gave-away-a-greater-percentage-of-their-income-during-the-great-depression-than-they-do-today/.

28. "Generation Anxious: Gen Z More Prone to Fear, Uncertainty Than Older Generations," Barna, October 1, 2024, https://www.barna.com/trends/generation-anxious-gen-z-more-prone-to-fear-uncertainty-than-older-generations/.

29. Lana Gillespie, "Bankrate's 2025 Annual Emergency Savings Report," Bankrate, March 26, 2025, https://www.bankrate.com/banking/savings/emergency-savings-report/.

30. Attributed to economist Eugene Fama.